RUN TO WIN

HOW TO ...
IMPROVE YOUR RUN INTO ETERNITY

Do you not know that those who run in a race all run, but one receives the prize?
Run in such a way that you may obtain it. (1 Cor 9:24 NKJV)

DAVID ROMERO

authorHOUSE®

AuthorHouse™
1663 Liberty Drive
Bloomington, IN 47403
www.authorhouse.com
Phone: 833-262-8899

Published by AuthorHouse 02/10/2021

ISBN: 978-1-6655-1632-7 (sc)
ISBN: 978-1-6655-1633-4 (hc)
ISBN: 978-1-6655-1634-1 (e)

Library of Congress Control Number: 2021902566

Print information available on the last page.

Scripture quotations marked KJV are from the Holy Bible, King James Version (Authorized Version). First published in 1611. Quoted from the KJV Classic Reference Bible, Copyright © 1983 by The Zondervan Corporation.

Scripture quotations marked NKJV are taken from the New King James Version. Copyright © 1982 by Thomas Nelson, Inc. Used by permission. All rights reserved.

My wife, Sheila, has displayed much patience and love toward me considering the time it has taken to develop this message. She showed her patience not just during my writing work, but most of all during the years I spent running, which enabled me to experience and develop this idea. Thanks for your support and the faith you have in me and the ideas expressed in this text.

Our two daughters, Monica and Aimee, have been examples of how God's grace and mercy can work, especially as Sheila and I had imperfect parenting skills when they arrived to form our family. Despite our struggles to parent effectively, they survived very well, correcting the mistakes we made with them as they raised their own children. God bless both of you!

I am not sure what kind of world my grandchildren and great-grandchildren will be living in. At this moment in time, is does not seem to be very encouraging for them. Faith in our Lord and Savior Jesus Christ is the most valuable possession they will need to complete the course that has been laid out for them. It is my hope they will seek the Lord with all their hearts as soon as possible before they need to do it out of desperation.

God bless each of my grandchildren:

Jared, Kyle, Lynette, Dani, and Randi.

God bless each of my great-grandchildren:

Kathryn, Isabella, Ashtyn,

Khylin, Kruz,

Braylon, Braylee, Laya, Laykon,

and Harper.

As an artist, I see a book as nothing more than a blank white canvas upon which the artist-writer paints images upon the minds of the readers with the brushstrokes of his words.

And thou shalt love the Lord thy God with all thy heart, and with all thy soul, and with all thy mind, and with all thy strength: this is the first commandment.

And the second is like, namely this, Thou shalt love thy neighbour as thyself. There is none other commandment greater than these. (Mark 12:30–31)

INTRODUCTION

You may never have thought of yourself as a runner, much less a marathon runner. The thought may even be repugnant to you as memories arise of high school physical education classes or some other sport you may have been coerced into playing. You may say, "I am not a runner and have no desire to be one." Or, "The idea is so foreign to me that it would take a miracle from heaven to make me change my mind."

The fact is, you are a long-distance runner whether the thought is appealing to you or not. We all run the race; however, we run different courses. You are running the course of life God has set you on. Here are some things to consider: Are you on that course, or have you taken a wrong turn along the way and are not sure where your original course is? Some people have been running for years off course, while others may not even know they have a given course to run. So why not consider getting back on course and running as efficiently as possible, avoiding the many obstacles along the way, and crossing the finish line strong.

For each of us, God has laid out a life course as He sees it. It is up to us to run it as best we can while giving close attention to the instruction He has provided. The paths this world offers continually add to the struggles we face daily. We don't know how long our course is or how treacherous it will be. God provides assistance when we become wise enough to seek it. Either way, we have been given a specific and personalized course to run.

Have you ever considered why you were born at this time in history? Why not two hundred years ago or two thousand years ago or even two hundred years into the future? None of these ideas happens because of mere chance. God is in control of the big picture and has created and equipped you for today. He has outfitted you with specific talents and abilities to enable you to fit in our society today. He knew you from before creation and chose to place you in today as He created the big picture of time. David wrote these words: "What is man, that thou art mindful of him?" (Psalm 8:4).

God had you in mind before you were conceived. He has a path with specific tasks and challenges for you to accomplish along your trek. In Psalm 139: 13–18 we read:

> For thou hast possessed my reins: thou hast covered me in my mother's womb.
>
> I will praise thee; for *I am fearfully and wonderfully made: marvellous are thy works; and that my soul knoweth right well.*
>
> My substance was not hid from thee, when I was made in secret, and curiously wrought in the lowest parts of the earth.
>
> *Thine eyes did see my substance, yet being unperfect; and in thy book all my members were written, which*

in continuance were fashioned, when as yet there was none of them.

How precious also are thy thoughts unto me, O God! how great is the sum of them!

If I should count them, they are more in number than the sand: when I awake, I am still with thee.

He formed you in your mother's womb. He designed you with talents and abilities for a specific purpose, to be applied at this specific time in history. In other words, He has set you on a life path to run your specific course in order that His will for His kingdom will be established as you apply your personal touch to the world we live in.

As you may have experienced in high school physical education class, some of us run better than others. This can be a result of physical attributes or attitude (or a combination of these). Desire to do our best or to discover our God-given talents can be a challenge so early in life. As adults, we should develop a responsible perspective of putting the needs all around us together with our given abilities.

So how can the physical challenges of a long-distance run compare to following the spiritual course God has placed us on? We will examine these ideas later in more detail. For now, we can certainly agree that some of us are off the course we have been set on, while others may be right on. With this rationale, we can conclude that we are, in fact, all runners with a given ability to choose how we will run once our feet hit the ground. We can choose to run the way God intended, having our feet clad with the gospel, pounding the pavement to build and make a difference in His kingdom, or we can choose to run the way that has been easy and more attractive to society and our own reasoning.

If you think you may be off course, what should you do to get back on based on God's design for your life? Only He has the answer to that question. We must develop a desire to seek His training and personal coaching, allowing it to be our directing force. Some runners have no clue about God's Word while others choose purposely to avoid it. If a runner sits on the couch with a bag of chips watching the big screen, not much will be accomplished in terms of being able to run a stronger race in the natural world. The same is true for the spiritual world. We must constantly feed our spirit with the "bread of life" instead of junk food. In the same aspect, we should exercise our spirits daily. Our spiritual runs in our spiritual bodies can closely parallel any physical runs in our physical bodies that we may attempt. In both cases, our feet must be on the ground running. Let us consider this idea a little deeper.

God has blessed my spiritual eyes and my physical body in such a way that I can see how He has worked with me and continues to do so. I believe He wants to work with everyone in a similar way. I was a competitive runner for over twenty years. During that same period, as a side note, I also worked in pottery extensively. As I studied God's Word, both experiences began to reveal to me an extended and detailed analogy of how His hands have been working in my life. My hope is that, as we look at the parallels I see between a serious runner and the analogy Paul used in Corinthians, you too may be able to look back and see how God has been working with you.

My challenge to you is this: As you read, examine your past while focusing on your God-given skills to determine if you can see how (and if) his hands have been working in your life.

I realize many of you have never been runners to the degree I have. With that assumption, I will attempt to explain running terminology as best I can and develop the analogy for you to understand. If you are familiar with some of the jargon or may be able to teach me a few more things about running, please be patient. I want to assure you that, as much as you will read about running in this text, my focus is not about running physically; rather, it is about how well we can run in our spirit. We all run physically and spiritually parallel through the realm of time directly into eternity. If we are all required by our Creator to make that run, then why not run as well as we can with the right objective seeking an eternal reward?

CHAPTER 1

RUN THE RACE

Again, you might say, "I'm not a runner, and I will never run a race." Remember that we are talking about comparing your life to a long run. The only choice you have is how to best accomplish it. Whether you can metaphorically run or just struggle your way through life, it is generally a long course that has only one primary objective: finishing well. Paul painted this same analogy in the minds of the Corinthian believers in the following passage:

> Know ye not that they which *run in a race* run all, but one *receiveth the prize*? So run, that *ye may obtain.*
>
> And every man that *striveth for the mastery* is *temperate in all things*. Now they do it to obtain a *corruptible crown*; but we *an incorruptible.*
>
> I therefore so run, not as uncertainly; so fight I, *not as one that beateth the air*:
>
> But I *keep under my body*, and *bring it into subjection*: lest that by any means, when I have

preached to others, I myself should be a castaway.
(1 Corinthians 9:24–27)

Paul was addressing the believers in the church of Corinth, Greece, when he wrote these words. The picture he drew in their minds was designed to demonstrate a very real-life comparison that is still applicable to us today—believers and nonbelievers alike. I will address specific elements of his analogy as we work through this study, and I'll simultaneously build a new one around our modern-day marathon race.

The culture of Paul's day was seriously involved in organized athletic competitions. These ancient games were the model for our contemporary Olympics. This era lasted from approximately 776 BC to AD 393, putting Paul in the middle of it.

The common belief of how and when the marathon started is based on a battle that took place in 490 BC between Greek and Persian soldiers in the land known as Marathon. Greatly outnumbered, the Greek soldiers defeated the Persians. To announce the great victory, a soldier named Pheidippides shed his armor and ran twenty-six miles from the battleground to Athens without stopping. The story is that he announced the victory before collapsing and dying.

Paul wanted the believers of the church in Corinth to know that they were living their lives with reason and purpose, anticipating a reward at the end of it all. He built his analogy around experiences they could relate to and identify with. He compared their lives of faith in Jesus to the disciplined and competitive world that was around them.

Let us turn our attention to the world you and I live in and ask this question: Is it fair to say that the life we live is like a marathon?

Many of us will answer this question by saying, "Yes, since life is long with many challenges along the way." Others may push back and say, "I do not want to be another Pheidippides. You may have to sell me on that one." That is my objective, grounded in my experiences.

We live on a planet that has been corrupted and cursed by the sin of humanity through Adam. By inheritance, that sin has guaranteed us countless obstacles and many hills to climb before we cross the finish lines of our lives. We run our races in the context of sin pushing against us like a strong headwind. Our mission is to arrive at our finish lines in blameless condition, by way of God's grace.

If you have not been a student of the Bible, you might think life was designed to be difficult. The truth is that God designed humans to have heavenly walks with Him through eternity—comparable to what most serious runners would consider a fun run. Such a run is short; it may include the runner's choice of walking, running, or jogging, with little to no stress on the body. It is just an enjoyable time with others. That was the type of relationship Adam enjoyed with his Creator until God gave him just one command: "But of the tree of the knowledge of good and evil, thou shalt not eat of it: for in the day that thou eatest thereof thou shalt surely die" (Genesis 2:17).

A jealous Satan was listening and put together an attractive deception. We know what happened. Adam believed Satan's trickery, and the sin of humanity that resulted put God's plan on a detour through a challenging and dangerous neighborhood. Because of Adam's sin, you and I are born into a very hostile environment. We are in peril and away from God's initial plan.

God revealed the difficulty we would face in life with these early words He spoke to Adam:

> And unto Adam he said, because thou hast hearkened unto the voice of thy wife, and hast eaten of the tree, of which I commanded thee, saying, Thou shalt not eat of it: cursed is the ground for thy sake; in sorrow shalt thou eat of it all the days of thy life;
>
> Thorns also and thistles shall it bring forth to thee; and thou shalt eat the herb of the field;
>
> In the sweat of thy face shalt thou eat bread, till thou return unto the ground; for out of it wast thou taken: for dust thou art, and unto dust shalt thou return. (Genesis 3:17–19)

Life has been that way since and is daily growing worse. The perils we face in the twenty-first century resemble the world described in Psalm 91 by Moses. We can almost hear these headlines on the evening news:

> Thou shalt not *be afraid for the terror by night;*
> nor for *the arrow that flieth by day;*
> Nor for *the pestilence that walketh in darkness;*
> nor for *the destruction that wasteth at noonday.*

*A thousand shall fall at thy side, and ten thousand
at thy right hand; but it shall not come nigh thee.*
(Psalm 91:5–7)

The world we live in is much more complicated with endless distractions and deceptions entangled with the advancement of technology. As bad as it was for Moses, the probable author of Psalm 91, the world seemed to be less gray then than it is today. We will go into a more detailed discussion in chapter 6 about the condition of the course we presently run.

Is there someone like Moses available to guide us through the dangers of today? The answer is yes—but even better. The saving grace of Jesus is obtainable by faith to do just that. When He left Earth, He sent His spirit to safely escort us through the hazards of today's world and lead us directly into His eternal kingdom. By our faith and the coaching of His spirit, we can develop a methodical desire to hear and cling to His commands. By way of His faith-producing Word, directed by His Spirit, we can run our races with confidence into the everlasting presence of God.

Even with the assistance of the Holy Spirit, the course we run is not an easy one. Many people work long and hard to provide the bare necessities for themselves and their families. Too few appreciate the blessings and opportunities available to us because we were born in this country. Not enough of us have had the opportunity to compare our blessings to those in the world who lack basic necessities in life. Our citizenship in the United States is a genuine blessing from heaven. People from other countries run a more treacherous course through life. Satan has consistently increased his deceptive activities and is working overtime to derail God's plan for the entirety of humankind.

We should value the talents and personality traits that have been placed in us by our Creator. Our gifts are specifically designed for our runs. If we apply these as God intended, then success in life is attainable. Success as defined by the world and our society is simply an accumulation of resources. If we apply our God-given abilities under His leadership, then we will succeed according to His definition of success. His viewpoint is the only one that counts. Without exception, He is the only official in the race we call life.

God has placed us on our courses at His chosen time, designed by His hand, so His spirit can, by relationship, supply His energy to our daily needs. We are His creations designed to serve His purposes.

In the book of John, we read that Nicodemus came to Jesus knowing He had been sent from God. He knew this because of the teachings and miracles Jesus did daily. He asked Jesus to tell him the means of obtaining eternal life. Jesus went directly to the heart of the matter and gave him an unexpected answer. I believe this was much more than Nicodemus was expecting.

Each of us has been given a course to run here on earth. At some point on that run, Jesus expects us to transition into eternity prior to crossing the finish line. Sooner is better than later. If you have made the transition Jesus speaks about in the book of John, you are a new creature running your course under His power instead of with your own ability. If not, then you need to seek Him out as Nicodemus did.

John described Nicodemus's encounter with Jesus this way:

> There was a man of the Pharisees, named Nicodemus, a ruler of the Jews:
>
> The same came to Jesus by night, and said unto him, Rabbi, we know that thou art a teacher come from God: for no man can do these miracles that thou doest, except God be with him.
>
> Jesus answered and said unto him, Verily, verily, I say unto thee, *Except a man be born again, he cannot see the kingdom of God.*
>
> Nicodemus saith unto him, How can a man be born when he is old? Can he enter the second time into his mother's womb, and be born?
>
> Jesus answered, Verily, verily, I say unto thee, *Except a man be born of water and of the Spirit, he cannot enter into the kingdom of God.*
>
> That which is born of the flesh is flesh; and that which is born of the Spirit is spirit.
>
> Marvel not that I said unto thee, Ye must be born again. (John 3:1–7)

This is the way I perceive God created us to run our races: By God's own personnel touch, humans are the only created beings who, by faith, can be recreated, reoriented, and revitalized to achieve their God-given potential, empowering them to finish their race highly favored.

Jesus told Nicodemus that man must be "born again" of the

Spirit. This rebirth is accomplished only by faith in the price Jesus paid on the cross for the sin of all humankind. Adam's sin as well as yours and mine were paid for by Jesus's blood, death, and resurrection.

In our analogy, a runner pays an entry fee to participate in a race. Jesus paid the entry fee on our behalf because we all start bankrupt. It is payment for our liberation from spiritual death. The fee was so great we could never have paid the price. The Bible says, "The wages of sin is death" (Romans 6:23). The price of all sin has been paid for by Jesus. Our responsibility is to personally accept His payment and show up to complete the race He has set before us. Completing our race without proof of His payment puts us in position for immediate disqualification.

So how do we run? And will anyone help? The answer to both questions is that God's Word is the guide. God has seen to it that His Word has been documented to be like a "training program" for our longest runs: our lives. It chronicles His dos and don'ts in such a way that we are enabled to run successfully following His directions and example.

He sent His Holy Spirit to become our personal trainer to coach us through the endurance of life's trials. We must accept Him and submit to His lordship; otherwise, crossing the finish line will yield eternal hopelessness. He wants to guide us through our course with confidence, as we learn to listen and trust Him.

I call Him our "Holy Coach." I have been under the direction of different coaches in the past. A good one will push you to excel. The Holy Spirit is no exception. Following His instruction puts us in position for spiritual success.

I have lived long enough to look back and see where God has protected me in my life run. The path He has guided me onto has protected me from many failures. He is a faithful God, and I must act upon the faith His Word provides. If I stay on course with His direction, He will lead me to certain victory. He has always been there to help and faithfully apply mercy to my failures.

When I was born again, life took on a different perspective for me. I was a new person. My spirit was alive with God's energy moving in me. I began to realize He had made me unique with a personality and talents woven into the person I call "me." That insight gave me a sense of responsibility and accountability for all He had provided. The course I am running has been an incredible journey, and I would like to share specific parts of it with you.

I was a serious runner for the better part of twenty-five years. Early on in this season of my life, I could see parallels in the way God was working on me. These years of physical running have opened my eyes to the way God wants to help us run spiritually through time, and into eternity with Him. My hope is that, by sharing these experiences, you will be able to see how he wants to assure your spiritual success. Failure should not be an option, but it can be if you make the wrong choice or, perhaps, no choice at all.

He is and will always be present to guide His family of believers. God asked Moses to speak these universal words to the Hebrew people, which also apply to us today: "I call heaven and earth to record this day against you, that I have set before you life and death, blessing and cursing: *therefore choose life*, that both thou and thy seed may live (Deuteronomy 30:19).

CHAPTER 2

A 26.2-MILE CHALLENGE LEADING INTO ETERNITY

For most people, life can easily be compared to a marathon, which is 26.2 miles long. Consider that distance and the time you will spend on your feet carrying your weight forward nonstop until the finish line is crossed. Some will dread the thought of doing such a thing and cringe at the amount of preparation necessary to do it successfully. If you have ever attempted to meet a challenge of this type, you will understand the comparison I am making in this text.

Depending at which stage of life you find yourself, you may look at the analogy somewhat differently. Let us consider the spiritual and the physical side by side throughout this analogy.

If you are young, you may underestimate the skill and discipline needed to successfully complete a run of this distance along with the endurance it requires. The physical condition a person needs to be in is intense; anything less could be hazardous. We will look at the spiritual comparison in the next few paragraphs.

When I was a young teen, I loved to run. I loved to challenge myself. I even made small weights to tie to my ankles during a run just for fun and to build endurance. I enjoyed the solitary time on the road. This was in the 1950s when life was much simpler. Running at school in sports and around the neighborhood was the only running I was familiar with. I had never heard of a marathon. I wonder what I would have done had I been familiar with it. Back then, long distances beyond the mile run were never considered. I had run many miles at my own pace for my own enjoyment, but never in competition. I had no understanding of the potential that resided within my body.

The same can be said for the spiritual life of many young people today. Many have no knowledge of the course they are on, the training they will need, or even the untapped ability that lies within them. Coaching wisdom is readily available to them if they would seek it. They have little understanding of the perils that lie ahead and the spiritual potential that can, by faith, carry them through to the end. Only through their right choices concerning faith can that aptitude be fully developed into skills for true life.

If you are middle aged, you may have already concluded that you should have taken the challenge of your life run more seriously. The longer we have lived, the more opportunities we have had to make wrong turns off the path God has laid before us. Some of the obstacles we face are placed before us as societal norms; others are a result of our own bad choices. Our courses through life have a way of revealing the degree of importance we should have considered from the very start. The earlier we come to that realization, the quicker we can return to our God-given course and apply His strength to the test. The closer we get to the end of our race, the more we need to lean into the faith of who He is, so we don't become weary. Our mission is to keep going, day by day, step by step. Paul said it this way:

> Wherefore take unto you the whole armour of God, that ye may be able to *withstand in the evil day*, and *having done all, to stand.*
>
> *Stand* therefore, having your loins girt about with truth, and having on the breastplate of righteousness;
>
> And *your feet shod with the preparation of the gospel* of peace. (Ephesians 6:13–15)

If you are not sure where you stand with your Creator who entered you in this race, know this: it is never too late to start seeking His direction—never. God meets you where you are, no matter your spiritual condition. If you have been beaten up and discarded by the horrible world system we live in, He can take you as you are and put you on the path to be a world-class runner. With your cooperation, He can activate your talents and abilities in such a way that you will run according to His design for your life. This is only possible when we totally submit to His coaching and lordship. Only He knows our full potential and how much time still exists before we cross our finish line.

If your finish line is in sight, there is still much hope. As a runner runs a marathon, the mile markers seem to get further and further apart, but in our life runs, the reverse is true: birthdays seem to get closer and closer together. No matter the distance you may have already traveled, your marathon may seem more like a sprint, since it has all gone by so fast. Life is short, and eternity appears to reference itself as a point outside of time. It is hard to imagine that all of time exists inside of eternity, and at some point, time as we know it will be limitless. In the Bible, the brevity of life is spoken of in this way:

> For all flesh is as grass, and all the glory of man as the flower of grass. The grass withereth, and the flower thereof falleth away:
>
> But the word of the Lord endureth forever. And this is the word which by the gospel is preached unto you. (1 Peter 1:24–25)

If you still have your youth, or if you are struggling to hold on to some of it, one thing will surely happen. One morning you will wake up and say, "Where did it all go?" Now is the time to connect with eternity via the eternal life Jesus has purchased for you. If such a question has become relevant in your life, you should evaluate how much road seems to lie ahead and what God's plan is to have you use that span wisely. After all, if you have expressed your faith and made the connection with eternity, truly your eternal life has begun before your physical one has ended. Keep running; eternal life is just beginning.

Seasoned runners always assess how much effort is needed to complete their runs. Knowing your physical ability relative to the remaining distance in a race is crucial to finishing well. My thoughts are that, upon entering eternity, we may be asked: "How completely did you run the course I gave you?" Have you ever considered the idea of having to account for how well you ran your course?

At the very minimum, our challenge is to do as much as we can to accomplish our best on the road that remains. God will not only want us to account for our efforts; His desire is to lead the way.

Don't fret over past failures and lost time. God is the Creator of time and can certainly redeem the past to favor your current circumstances. Trust Him. He not only knows the way, He is the way through your remaining course.

The good thing about this analogy is that God has the perfect plan for your success, no matter what part of the road you find yourself on. According to Paul, we all run the race whether we follow God's plan or not. So why not run it His way, with His support, and finish respectably like a true world-class winner, not of this natural world, but of the spiritual realm!

Let us examine in detail the specifics of a successful marathon run as compared to a successful spiritual life well lived.

CHAPTER 3

EQUIPMENT NEEDED

Running is a very inexpensive activity and can be accomplished almost anywhere. All you need are a good pair of shoes, simple attire, and a safe place to run. Like any other sport, when we strive to have the latest and the best of the available extras, it can get rather expensive. Owning the latest and best does not guarantee success.

Shoes are the key ingredient to staying on your feet as comfortably as possible for the duration. They must be designed for the distance. They should fit well and be broken in. Good running shoes are light in weight and durable. Shoes are not the place to cut cost. Socks should not be an afterthought either. Be sure they fit the feet well. They shouldn't be too tight or too loose, which could cause blisters. Close attention to a good investment for your feet will greatly improve your ability to run successfully. Your feet and your shoes should function as one element. Some of the popular running shoes on the market today are Saucony Triumph, Reebok Forever Floatride Energy 2, Brooks Ghost, and Hoka Carbon X.

Feet are such an important part of our spiritual run that Paul did not fail to stress them in His analogy to the Ephesians: "And your feet shod with the preparation of the gospel of peace" (Ephesians 6:15).

In chapter 5, we will discuss how to invest the gospel into our daily training in such a way as to prepare our feet properly for the course we are running. This preparation is also an area where we should never cut costs. It is vital to our spiritual run and an area in which time and effort are well invested.

Our objective should be that, as our feet and shoes function as one, so should our daily lives function as one with the Word of God. Our daily living should reflect the semblance of Jesus.

As you run and train for a race of marathon proportions, you will want to face the challenge carrying as little weight as possible upon your body. Shirts, shorts, and socks need to be light and breathable upon your body. Every ounce of weight carried the distance of twenty-six miles requires a tremendous amount of energy. Seriously consider each ounce of burden.

In our spiritual run, the first weight we must strive to shed is the weight of sin. Sin is a tremendous load upon our bodies, minds, and spirits. It is the heaviest of all burdens we carry.

As we consider the weight of the clothes and shoes we wear during our runs, we need to seek out every speck of sin that may be holding us back from living a godly life. We need to strip down to the bare necessities and especially eliminate habits that are attached to unproductive aspects of our living, along with desires and driving forces that control our time and efforts daily. We must consider if any of these are leading our focus to God or perhaps helping our fellow humans. If they are not, we should consider them unproductive and just excess.

There are things we need and things we want. The things we want often become extra weight we carry once we have them. They become costly in money and time. Maintenance of these pointless items is often burdensome to the point of taking the focus off what God may want us to do.

The apostle Paul wrote this to the Galatian Church: "But let every man prove his own work, and then shall he have rejoicing in himself alone, and not in another. For *every man shall bear his own burden* (Galatians 6:4–5).

These words could not be better spoken to each of us today. The society we live in today emphasizes *things*: we should all have the biggest and the best, problem or not.

Salvation by faith in Jesus frees us from the sin load we bear prior to acquiring faith.

The process that happens after salvation takes place is a stripping down and stripping off of the burdens we carry. It is a sanctifying process, purifying and dedicated to the right motives. The sin burden is so heavy that it can eventually result in death to the person carrying it. The sooner we are free of those burdens, the healthier our life run becomes.

Paul continued his letter to the Galatians:

> Be not deceived; God is not mocked: for whatsoever a man soweth, that shall he also reap.
>
> For he that soweth to his flesh shall of the flesh reap corruption; but he that soweth to the Spirit shall of the Spirit reap life everlasting.
>
> And let us not be weary in well doing: for in due season we shall reap, if we faint not. (Galatians 6:7–9)

Jesus spoke similar words:

> Come unto me, all ye that labour and are heavy laden, and I will give you rest.
>
> Take my yoke upon you, and learn of me; for I am meek and lowly in heart: and ye shall find rest unto your souls.
>
> For *my yoke is easy, and my burden is light.* (Matthew 11:28–30)

When we place our faith in what Jesus has done for us, our spiritual runs are not overbearing; rather, we are enabled to progress despite the circumstances. When we run with Jesus, we run with the one who has already carried our burdens to the cross.

The society we live in has a way of attaching weights to us in deceptive ways. What was once the truth is today a lie, and what was once a lie is sold as the truth today. Satan and his influence upon this world have turned it upside-down. It is important for us to know Who the truth is today and where we can find Him.

When I was young, I added weights to my legs to build endurance. Unknowingly or by our choices, many of us have done the same thing, accumulating the weight of sin we carry as we live life. Training with weights can be helpful to build physical muscle, but the burdens of sin will always be a hinderance to our spirits. Such burdens do not build up anything; they tear everything down.

God has a better plan. As we become spiritually proficient in His Word, we are cultivated in our ability to use our circumstances and obstacles to build within us spiritual endurance. Following His Word, like lifting weights, becomes spiritual resistance to sin making the muscles of our spirits stronger. That resistance builds into us trust and wisdom. Any task in life will be better accomplished with the knowledge of God's Word guided by His Spirit. Therefore, having a copy of His instructions in the gospel with us at critical times becomes vital to running successfully. A good Bible should be part of our essential equipment. Learning to use it and applying its contents to our daily training program is an ongoing process, repeating Paul's warning where he said, "And your feet shod with the preparation of the gospel of peace" (Ephesians 6:15).

Our spiritual feet should function as one with the gospel. It is a one size fits all; while, at the same time, it is custom made and personal for each of us. Like shoes, socks, shirts, and shorts to the runner, the gospel well fitted upon us is critical to our Christian lives. It is not only for you and me; it is also for those we run next to. Our commission is to carry the knowledge of His Word into the entire world to those places the Holy Spirit leads us. Let us do this as efficiently and effective as possible, with reduced burden.

How much preparation have you made to run your race?

Arc you carrying excess weight?

Are circumstances creating resistance in your faith?

Have you let God properly outfit you to run efficiently?

CHAPTER 4

RACE DISTANCE

In this analogy that compares life with the marathon, our lives on Earth represent the longest race any of us will ever run. The distance of our lives is calculated incrementally by the measurement of years. We have a date of birth and a future date. Between these dates, we make our transition from the pressures of time into eternity. It is our responsibility to understand the probable length of time that will lapse in between our dates and to determine how well and for what purpose we will get the most out of it. None of us knows for sure how much time we have, and as we age, the remaining distance to the end of our time is shortened with the close of each day.

If we seek to improve how well we cover our remaining distance, we need to evaluate the gifts God has placed in us and how they can develop to be more effective. Many people complete their entire run through life with no genuine purpose; they just pound the pavement of time. Once we realize we have been given a specific place in time by our Creator, then it becomes easier to begin the search for His direction in our run. We are born with all the talents and abilities we need to succeed and, at the same time, contribute to the development of His kingdom on Earth. Realizing there is real life before and after crossing our finish line should give us motivation to seek His will and develop a desire to fulfill our potential.

Led by the norms of our society, some of us may be off the course God designed and desired for us. If we seriously evaluate where we are in our life run, we may possibly conclude we have been running in the wrong direction. Today's corruption hidden in confusion is Satan's design to have us running in circles like dogs chasing their tails. The forces of evil we face today are hyperactive in the skill of diversion, enabling time to pass by seemingly unnoticed. Running according to God's will connects us to His promises now and assures our spiritual afterlife with Him later. We will develop this idea again in a future chapter. Now we need to focus on our present course.

The extensive distance of this course affords most of us the time we need to evaluate where we are and what we have accomplished to this point. With the remaining time ahead, we need to reevaluate our priorities and adjust our plans to win according to God's wise direction.

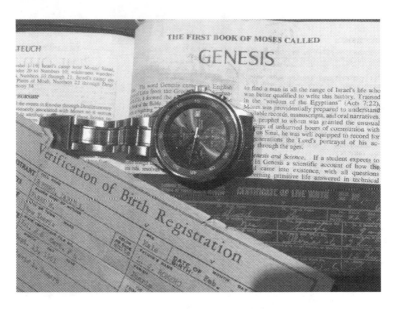

Many people who run through this life do not know that God has numbered our days. Only He is aware of the total allotted time we have. This inference is expressed in Psalm 90, believed to have been written by Moses:

> So *teach us to number our days*, that we may apply our hearts unto wisdom.
>
> Return, O LORD, how long? and let it repent thee concerning thy servants.
>
> O satisfy us early with thy mercy; that we may rejoice and *be glad all our days*.
>
> Make us glad according to the days wherein thou hast afflicted us, *and the years wherein we have seen evil*. (Psalm 90:12–15)

Our sinful secular world has a way of erecting signs to distract us and point us in the wrong direction. Satan is the author of confusion and is extremely effective at it. He deceived Eve in the garden and is still roaming Earth with his many followers doing the same. He has managed to warp our society so much that it is close to resembling Sodom and Gomorrah. His recruits in our culture run for the here and now of personal gain, directing blame and deception away from themselves. Unless their direction and purpose changes to running with the truth of God's Word, they will be lost forever. What could result is a waste of God's creative ability by the personal choices many have made.

The distance in our race is so many years long and requires such an effort daily that we should focus every bit of our energy on the fact that it will lead us ultimately face to face with our Creator. Most of us have enough time remaining to evaluate the "here and now" versus "eternity." Jim Elliot, with God-given wisdom said, "He is no fool who gives what he cannot keep, to gain what he cannot lose."[1] Jim and four others were killed by native Quechua Indians of Ecuador while ministering in the jungles of South America. He gave up what he could not hold on to: his life. He and the others gained eternity through their faith. In the years that past many of the natives he ministered to came to faith in Jesus Christ, including the one who killed him. His story is worth researching. For most of us, eternity seems so far away and out of sight. The reality is that we can step into eternity today by our faith in Jesus because He gave up His life for us personally.

---

[1] From the book by Irene Howat; Jim Elliot: He Is No Fool (Torchbearers)

The definitive wisdom of God's Word provides us with a lens that we should use to bring His guidance into focus. The direction and support He provides over the distance and time we are on Earth is critical to our runs being successful. We are all running our races at our own pace with or without God's help. At the same time, we are all running spiritually into eternity. Our earthly run has a starting line and a finish line. Our spiritual run has two starting lines, the first one at birth and the second one at the rebirth of our spirits. If we fail by our lack of faith to cross that second starting line at any point during our run, then we are disqualified for eternal reward. Do not miss out on the new start Jesus provides as we come to faith in Him.

No matter where you are in life or how off course you may be, God can draw a line in front of you today, designating your new spiritual starting line. If you have run for years without His help, He offers forgiveness and can redeem your unproductive time as you surrender to Him. To state it another way, He literally meets you where you are and places before you a fresh new start—if your faith is in Him and what He did for you: "Therefore if any man be in Christ, he is a new creature: old things are passed away; behold, all things are become new" (2 Corinthians 5:17).

We are all in the longest race we will ever struggle through. Running such a distance requires a specific and acquired endurance. Becoming a winner provides the reward of rest. In Him we become that winner and share eternal, never-ending rest.

Carefully consider this idea: We are all in the longest race we will ever run.

Have you experienced fatigue yet?

Do you know who offers you a new starting line and where to find it?

Have you placed your feet into eternity yet?

CHAPTER 5

TRAINING BASE

Running is an activity that intermixes our physical and mental conditioning. The marathon is of such duration and requires such physical conditioning that it will challenge anyone's ability and desire to keep running. Among well-trained runners, quitting is never an option.

It is important for long-distance runners to have built up a base of stamina capable of sustaining them through the distance of 26.2 miles. To cover such an expanse requires a plan of repetitious workouts that will take runners from where they are physically and then gradually build their endurance to a level at which they are able to run the distance nonstop. This takes months of training at gradually increased intensities. The goal is for this training to enable runners to build up to and incorporate several workouts of twenty miles nonstop. This should be a minimum target to achieve a few weeks prior to the designated race.

Effective workouts involve variations of short runs, gradually building up to longer distances, mixed in with interval runs.

Interval runs are nonstop at a training pace with spurts of speed for set distances mixed in.

At least one day off per week for recovery is necessary to avoid overtraining. This enables the body to rebuild itself. Consistency in such an intense training program is important to develop runners' confidence and trust in their physical condition before a race. A focus on efficiency of motion in the whole process is extremely vital to improve and retain muscular and lung development. Wasted or inefficient motion can lead to injury. The goal should be to never waste energy in workouts and races. Have other runners observe your motion of stride and make corrections accordingly. Make every motion count toward forward progress. Eliminate unproductive movement of the hands, arms, and legs. Paul stated this concept using these words: "I therefore so run, not as uncertainly; so fight I, *not as one that beateth the air*: But I *keep under my body*, and *bring it into subjection*" (1 Corinthians 9:26).

Forward travel should be in sync with every functioning part of the runner's body. Each physical movement should have a purpose in moving the runner's body forward towards the finish line. All wasted motion is just that: a useless waste of energy not available for the task when called upon.

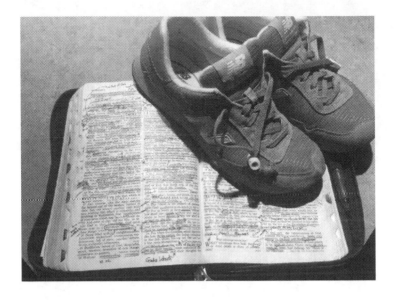

Let us revisit some previously used terms from the spiritual side. We all start our spiritual runs as beginners. Small steps grow into larger ones as we learn to grow in the knowledge of His Word. Short runs become doable before we build our stamina to achieve longer ones. Running in the Spirit progresses in much the same way as our physical running. As we commit ourselves to a base of learning God's direction for our lives, we grow directly in proportion to that effort.

As runners develop skill, they acquire the ability to do interval runs at a longer and faster pace. The practice of hill and bleacher running builds the strength needed to face spans of elevation along the course as well as other happenstances.

In a similar way, our spiritual growth will face periods of hard times, trouble, and seemingly impossible trials. Faithful believers often refer to these as peaks and valleys. Good training in God's Word gives us the ability to face the tests that frequently appear before us. Running out of any valley is a trial that will serve us well once we reach a peak. The valleys build in us the spiritual stamina required to keep running. Concurrently, they help us build a stronger trust in His ability to lead us out of the next valley. Almost assuredly, there will be another one we will have to face. Paul said we must be ready: "But I *keep under my body*, and *bring it into subjection*" (1 Corinthians 9:26b).

Serious runners through life must develop discipline, motivation, and persistence if these attributes do not already exist within. The Holy Spirit prepares our spirits to receive such masteries, and by faith, our flesh is trained to assist in their application. To paraphrase Paul, we must bring our bodies into subjection; in other words, we must be well trained.

If we permit, the Holy Spirit will develop godly character in us if we show a willingness to accept conviction and correction. To be successful, we must apply the correction that emanates from His training program, the Word. If we listen and follow His direction, our weaknesses are strengthened in its application. Commitment keeps us in the mode of seeking a godly way of life during these daily workouts of life. Just as we listen to a coach's voice, we need to develop a desire to hear His unbiased and holy direction no matter how much pain is involved. He is not only our Coach; if we allow, He becomes our Personal Trainer.

A race of this distance requires disciplined training and a good deal of sacrifice. Running a marathon means giving up a considerable amount of time we would ordinarily apply to another part of our lives. Discipline and commitment are the very ingredients necessary for success. This comparison illustrates the same effort we should apply to our spiritual run from where we are today forward into eternity.

For runners, various workout programs are available online or in running magazines. No matter the level of physical condition you may be in, there is a program for you out there. These are usually proven and can help you build a solid base of conditioning that will enable you to cross the finish line successfully and in good health. The program you choose should be based on your current physical condition and how much time you have before the actual race. Maintaining the self-discipline needed to follow your program will be as great a challenge as running the race itself. As a matter of fact, if you place a great deal of effort into following the training program, running the race will be much easier. There will always be circumstances that challenge your will to "stick to it" and get out and run. Life brings many distractions that can easily be converted into excuses. Motivation and persistence facilitate success in overcoming these distractions.

The good news is God's best workout program for our life race. No matter what spiritual condition we find ourselves in, He can and does get us through the finish line when we apply His Word as our workout. We must first accept the fact that he is the only one who can effectively coach us through our course because He has already run it in our place. Everything He did on Earth was for our benefit. He lived out His life so we would have a pattern to follow. God's Word is a program that fits all of us according to our needs. Training based on His life of perfection cannot fail us, because He did not fail.

I suggest you accept Him as your Coach while there are still miles ahead to run. The earlier in life you can commit to such a decision, the stronger your finish will be. His program for you is established in His Word, the Bible. The world offers many counterfeits, distractions, and assorted excuses for not seeking His program or for choosing not to follow it. Many of us know it is in our best interest but find excuses not to do it. A life of "faith" requires commitment to His principles which, in turn, develops character and self-control. In a similar way to a commitment to train for a marathon, your commitment to His program will develop faith stamina crucial to your race. Sound godly character develops the strong suit needed to reject distractions and temptations on the corrupt materialistic course you run.

Paul, knew we needed a sound training base to run our race successfully. He stated this concept to Timothy in these words: "Study to shew thyself approved unto God, a workman that needeth not to be ashamed, rightly dividing the word of truth" (2 Timothy 2:15).

The ideal situation in preparing for our race is to have a good coach. I have had several in school and at work. Many of us have participated in sports or have worked under the direction of a trainer or coach. A good one will put you through test that will enable you to evaluate your strengths and weaknesses. Those observations will determine weak areas that need more development, thus directing the coach to customize a program fit for the desired result. By building and working on your various flaws, the coach grows you repeatedly towards a desired purpose.

When I started running, it was not to run a marathon or, essentially, any race; it was to drop weight and get in better physical condition. I was running for almost five years before I ran in my first race. I did it because the company I worked for was a sponsor and asked me to participate. Because of the foundation I had already established through my jogging, I surprised myself by completing the five miles in forty-five minutes.

There were many people watching that race. Similarly, in life, others are always watching. We often set an example to others when we have no intention of doing so. Audiences of any type will cause an additional flow of adrenaline in runners, delivering an extra boost of energy when needed. The wise and well-trained runners know how to control and use this burst of energy resourcefully. We will discuss this idea again in subsequent chapters.

Our spiritual run requires strength and stamina in our faith, developed upon sound knowledge of God's Word. In Romans Paul stated, "So then faith cometh by hearing, and hearing by the word of God" (Romans 10:17).

In the same way as our physical bodies run on caloric intake, our spiritual bodies—our "spirits"—run on cultivated faith. We can keep our physical bodies fueled with healthy food to help us overcome the challenges in a race. Likewise, we should keep our spirits fueled with God's Word to help us overcome the challenges of life.

The terrain of life offers resistance and obstacles that help us build this faith base on strength and endurance. By faith, and the repetitive application of it to our daily life, our Coach (the Holy Spirit) takes us from where we are spiritually and begins to grow in us God's designed purpose. The daily exercise of our faith enables this spiritual process to mature in strength and endurance. His

Word is the spiritual fuel we need to power our daily endurance on the course we run. Isaiah best expressed this idea with the following words:

> Whom shall he teach knowledge? and whom shall he make to understand doctrine? them that are weaned from the milk and drawn from the breasts.
>
> *For precept must be upon precept, precept upon precept; line upon line, line upon line; here a little, and there a little:*
>
> For with stammering lips and another tongue will he speak to this people.
>
> To whom he said, *This is the rest* wherewith ye may cause the weary to rest; and *this is the refreshing:* yet they would not hear. (Isaiah 28:9–12)

Precept upon precept, line upon line: these are repeated twice in case we miss them the first time or fail to realize they are important. Repetition leading to higher levels is a fundamental for building strength and stamina both physically and spiritually. His Word is the base for our training program to develop fit spirits. As in verse twelve above, today not many hear or even try to hear. Let us who hear work out fervently to build strength in our spirits! When we follow our Coach's lead by hearing the Word of God, faith comes and builds a genuine spiritual determination and direction within us: "I will run the way of thy commandments, when thou shalt enlarge my heart. Teach me, O Lord, the way of thy statutes; and I shall keep it unto the end" (Psalm 119:32–33).

Trials and tragedies in life will test the faith stamina we have acquired. Applying faith in a daily disciplined and consistent measure helps us build the footing upon which we can run. We must not only run; we must run persuasively to the finish.

The peaks and valleys we face in life challenge us the way training intervals challenge runners. Intervals strengthen a runners' speed and endurance. When we keep a strong commitment to focus on God's workout plan, He in turn provides periods of much-needed rest for our souls. Our spirits need restorative rest with Him to rebuild themselves in the same way our bodies need rest.

Serious training is vital for a run of this duration.

How committed are you in your lifelong race?
Are you interested in improving the excellence of your running?
Have you sought a superior training plan to please your Coach?

CHAPTER 6

KNOWLEDGE OF THE COURSE

For such a distance as a marathon, it is important to know the course you will be running. Will it be flat or hilly? What are the average daytime temperatures at the time of year you will be running? Is it in an urban or rural area? What is the altitude? Are there other significant aspects of this route?

Your workouts should be designed to incorporate all characteristics and challenges you might find along that run. If you have completed the course before, much of the guesswork becomes working knowledge of the type of training that will work best considering your last effort. With no experience on the course, you can consult others who have previously run the race and have a working knowledge of its unique challenges. Do not be afraid to ask those who may know. Preparing is always better than being caught unaware. The worst possible thing that can happen is that you are running well and feeling good about the whole run but then you begin to question in your mind: *Am I on the correct course or have I taken a wrong turn by following others who didn't know the correct way?*

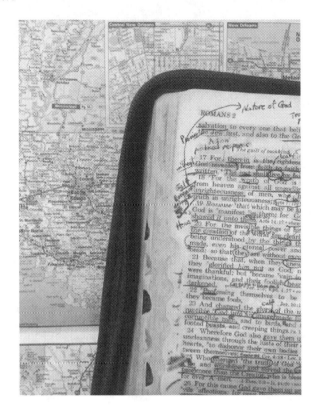

Let us look at the challenges that you and I face along the course we presently run. It is ever changing, seemingly for the worse. If you have run now for any number of years, you can certainly relate to this. The course we run today is extremely depraved compared to the course of thirty to fifty years ago. It can best be compared to a primitive cesspool. The elements we are subjected to and must navigate through are filthy. The mess in our society today was well documented in the Bible over two thousand years ago. It is as if Paul was listening to our evening news as he wrote the following letter to Timothy:

> This know also, that in the last days *perilous times shall come.*
>
> For *men shall be lovers of their own selves, covetous, boasters, proud, blasphemers, disobedient to parents, unthankful, unholy,*
>
> *Without natural affection, trucebreakers, false accusers, incontinent, fierce, despisers of those that are good,*
>
> *Traitors, heady, highminded, lovers of pleasures* more than lovers of God;
>
> Having *a form of godliness, but denying the power thereof*: from such turn away.
>
> For of this sort are *they which creep into houses, and lead captive silly women laden with sins, led away with divers lusts,*
>
> *Ever learning, and never able to come to the knowledge of the truth.*
>
> Now as Jannes and Jambres withstood Moses, so do *these also resist the truth: men of corrupt minds, reprobate concerning the faith.*
>
> But they shall proceed no further: for *their folly shall be manifest unto all men*, as theirs also was. (2 Timothy 3:1–9)

Do you agree with me that what is stated in this scripture is exactly what we are exposed to in today's godless society? So many people are their own gods or have constructed their god to reflect their own desire. This is the treacherous course of the society we find ourselves in today. The directional signs on that course point in the wrong direction. For the most part, so many people's way is designed to please themselves. It points them away from God and into trouble. It is almost as if we have been placed in an environment that offers no hope. We should be careful not to venture into that neighborhood unaware. In and of itself, the world has no hope, but Paul offered the help we need to find our way through this sin laden wasteland: "But thou hast fully known my *doctrine, manner of life, purpose, faith, longsuffering, charity, patience*" (2 Timothy 3:10).

Paul experienced the gospel face to face in the presence of Jesus. He soon learned that, as he followed Jesus, he was sure to find the correct course for his life. Jesus pointed the way, and Paul became the experienced runner who offered his knowledge and experience to Timothy. Paul trained him in the sound doctrine of faith and the fruit within the life he lived and demonstrated. What was true for Timothy then is even more critical for us to lean on today. The recorded words of Jesus and Paul give us "the way" we are to run through the dangerous neighborhoods of life today. It is as if God, by inspiration, gave to the authors of the Bible a type of modern-day GPS we can use to navigate through these hazards.

Being able to recognize the depth of distraction and perversion along the course we run may not seem important, but it does offer advantages. As we face potholes in our paths, the Word of

God helps us understand when to leap over and when simply navigate around such potential mishaps. Living victoriously in this godless society can only be achieved by rightly appreciating Jesus and being guided by His precepts. With that knowledge, believers need to recognize He has provided His Holy Spirit to run alongside us, directing our every step. As I have previously declared, He positions Himself as our Coach, and only He knows what is around the next corner or even the distance remaining to our finish line. The trust we build in His coaching ability becomes crucial to our daily and lifetime success.

Jesus gave us the pattern in which we should pray for daily guidance: "Thy kingdom come. Thy will be done in earth, as it is in heaven" (Matthew 6:10). You and I run our races the total distance only one time. There are no do-overs. Once we cross the finish line, there is no possibility we can do it again. Therefore, in this life, we must seek all the guidance God has provided in His Word. Being "born again" gives us that new starting line in the run we started at birth. With this new start, He provides us an extraordinary opportunity to spiritually begin afresh. The following are the words Paul used to describe this truth: "Therefore if any man be in Christ, he is a new creature: old things are passed away; behold, all things are become new" (2 Corinthians 5:17).

Our natural birth does not afford us such a luxury. Without the power of this spiritual new start, we may find ourselves in repetitive situations which often open the opportunity for habitual sin to establish a stronghold in our lives. Our old spirits from our first birth are ones of death and have no power to resist our struggles with the culture of today.

We need to constantly be asking ourselves these questions: "Am I on the correct course according to God's will for my life? Do I know where this course is taking me? Do I have the humility to ask forgiveness and ask Him to direct me back to the course designed specifically for me?

Thank God our Coach is a forgiving one who desires to help us through each minute and each mile of life's challenges. Our objective should be to learn from each event we encounter—what happened and why. God gives us the opportunity to be somewhat selfish with His Word. We should always ask: What does His Word say in view of my circumstances, and what can I learn from its application? We should study and grow through all the circumstances we experience. If sin has produced such an event, and we sincerely confess it, our Coach is there to guide us to a higher level of faithful endurance. In the book of John, John wrote what Jesus said: "These things I have spoken unto you, that in me ye might have peace. In the world ye shall have tribulation: but be of good cheer; I have overcome the world" (John 16:33).

In this comparison, our Coach has overcome the world (the course you and I run.) As deplorable as our society has become, He has conquered it at its worst. He has navigated all the challenges human life has, and He offers His experience and knowledge for our use. He is the only one who has run the race in perfection. He has experienced all the resistance and challenges we might face, and more. Our relationship with Him must be based on the trust that He will share with us His strategies for success. Our part is to believe and continue our run confidently in faith on the course He wants to lead us through.

Even though we are still running the race, He sees us as having previously crossed the finish line strong! Faith in Him while seeking His guidance is sufficient for all the difficulties ahead.

Paul faced many obstacles in his run, but he found trust in the words of Jesus when he spoke to the church in Corinth: "And he said unto me, My grace is sufficient for thee: *for my strength is made perfect in weakness.* Most gladly therefore will I rather glory in my infirmities, that the *power of Christ* may rest upon me" (2 Corinthians 12:9).

By running daily with Him, we can look back over time and see the places and events He has directed us out of, away from, or through. As it was with Paul, many obstructions and circumstances still lie in our paths:

> I know both how to be abased, and I know how to abound: everywhere and in all things I am instructed both to be full and to be hungry, both to abound and to suffer need.
>
> *I can do all things through Christ which strengtheneth me.*
>
> Notwithstanding ye have well done, that ye did communicate with my affliction. (Philippians 4:12–14)

In so many ways, our world has become so dark that we need a spiritual flashlight to make our way through the social deceptions. His Word provides just that light by the truth it represents: "Through thy precepts I get understanding: therefore I hate every false way. *Thy word is a lamp unto my feet, and a light unto my path"* (Psalm 119:104–105).

Do you have the wisdom and truth necessary for the challenges the world system has placed before you? Jesus said this: "Then said Jesus to those Jews which believed on him, If ye continue in my word, then are ye my disciples indeed; And ye shall know the truth, and the truth shall make you free" (John 8:31–32).

There is only way to acquire truth, and that is from God himself by His Word. Wisdom is knowing how to apply truth into our daily runs with Him.

Meditate upon corrections you may have to make along your way.

Seek His desired course for your life and discard the world options you may be trapped in.

Are you pursuing direction according to God's truth or the world's truth?

Are you anxious about course corrections His Word may require you to make?

CHAPTER 7

PACING YOURSELF

Critical to all runners is the honest knowledge of their physical condition. Overconfidence and the increase of adrenaline from excitement can be critical in a race of this distance. Too much energy used too early in the race leaves less for the final miles.

You should start conservatively, reserving strength for the more demanding miles ahead. Be confident with your training pace and resist the temptation to follow the herd of runners. Your best run will be achieved at a steady pace you are familiar with. It's easy to get caught up in the adrenaline flow and exhilaration of the moment and forget your overall game plan. The sound of the starter gun and the initial movement of the runners can be very enticing at the start. Focus on your pace and settle into that groove as soon as possible. I speak from the experience of having run sixteen marathons, each in a reasonable time, and all finished in good condition. Knowledge of what you can and cannot do is essential to running as a winner. There is plenty of time to pick up the pace once you are sure you can physically hold it for the entire distance. In the last few miles, I always found myself in need of every micron of energy my body had in reserve. To make it across the finish line strong, I realized I had to have a steady and unrelenting pace that closely paralleled my intensity of training.

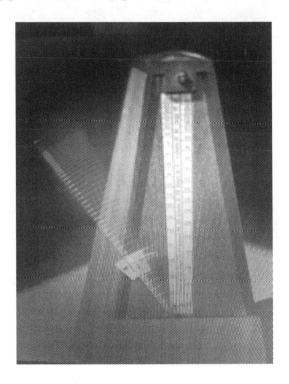

A steady and fluid pace—like the ticking of a metronome—churns out a tremendous advantage in most runners. Inconsistent training with an inconsistent pace can draw out the time it takes to get the conditioning base needed and often leaves the runner with these questions in mind: Am I ready to take this on? Can I do this? On the other hand, training with a consistent focus on a smooth rhythm and a steady pace develops in a runner the peace and confidence that says I can do this! Then the questions remaining are: Can this race be a personal best for me? Can I better my best time?

Spiritually, it is critical for believers to know their footing with God. Pride and ego can easily get in the way to cause overconfidence. Daily study with consistent research in His Word provides a steady growth in faith. Assuming you know more about how God wants you to live out your life can easily lead to a false sense of assurance. Humility to self and focus on God leads to balance and consistency that will serve believers nicely. If we make any assumptions, they should be that we never know enough and there is always more to learn.

As faith runners, we should be listening to our Coach and following His training plan, His Word. We should ask these questions: Have I established a place in my daily routine where I can focus on Him and hear His instruction? Am I setting the pace, or am I trusting my Coach to do that for me? These questions are spiritually important.

It's easy to find ourselves in prideful situations in which we think, *Anyone can do this. I can handle this.* God's Word teaches us to recognize when we are operating in our "self-directed flesh" instead of seeking His lead along the way. We must be obedient to His pace and let Him be the frontrunner. If we find ourselves in a place that is outside of His lead, we should repent and run back toward Him swiftly. Our training should be essentially based on a Word-controlled and consistent workout according to His Holy Spirit. Paul said it this way: "And every man that *striveth for the mastery* is *temperate in all things*" (1 Corinthians 9:25).

The interpreter of Paul's statement uses the word *temperate* here to emphasize the concept of self-control. *Discipline* is another word we could use. The discipline and self-control we develop in our lives are achieved best through the power of His Spirit that is alive in us. As true followers of Jesus, we must not only be skilled in quoting His Word; we must apply it with each step we take consistently in the "workout" of our daily lives.

Some of us have the personality and energy of someone who is always on the go. Others are more laid back, and some critically need resuscitation. None of these traits work very well when we consider what many people believe is necessary in life to be successful. A disciplined, well-paced approach to our run will, in most cases, serve us well over the years and miles of life. A good pace well-coordinated will serve believers well.

I believe God is seeking a constant and steady improvement in our daily relationship with Him and the confidence to finish strong. Our strength is developed through reading His Word and having daily meetings with Him, our Coach, one on one. He provides guidance and reassurance. He is there to take us through it all. This wisdom of having a steady pace was given to Solomon in these words: "*The race is not to the swift*" (Ecclesiastes 9:11).

Our races should be set at an unfailing and calculated pace with and in Him. Inconsistency in His Word prolongs the time we need to build our required enduring faith base. It also robs us of the power we need to run. Paul emphasized this in his letter written to the Ephesians: "Now unto him that is able to do exceeding abundantly above all that we ask or think, according to the power that worketh in us" (Ephesians 3:20).

As critical as it is to know our physical condition for running, it is even more important for us to know our spiritual condition for living to the max. Life is a marathon event we cannot avoid. We are all born into it by God's will. One question we should always ask ourselves is: How important is it to have God guide my steps along this way? In offering the answer, I will repeat this scripture I presented earlier because it makes the point:

> Whom shall he teach knowledge? and whom shall he make to understand doctrine? them that are weaned from the milk, and drawn from the breasts.
>
> For precept must be upon precept, precept upon precept; line upon line, line upon line; here a little, and there a little. (Isaiah 28:9–10)

This scripture suggests a steady progression of growth with a workout pace that allows time for application of what has been learned. We all start as new babes and grow to the point where we can feed ourselves on His teachings This leads to more growth and eventual maturity.

Too much speed applied too early in the marathon can lead to burnout or injury. In our spiritual run, a steady, consistent, and guided pace most assuredly will lead to our eternal victory.

Examine your commitment to His guidance a bit further.

Have you established a pace that is challenging yet not injurious to your growth in Him?

Do you have confidence and peace in your spirit to finish your run with victory?

Have you established discipline to run again and again following your Coach's lead?

CHAPTER 8

SUPPORT ALONG THE WAY

Having a support team is vital to all runners. Although it is somewhat a solitary sport, spouses, family members, friends, and community members can really do a lot to cheer runners on. Faith in one's ability and encouragement from others along the way are almost always vital to success. In this quest, runners almost always run alone as their bodies respond to their level of preparation. The marathon is not a team sport. There can be thousands of runners around you. They will all be running their own race unless you have arranged for a friend to encourage and guide you. One face recognized in the crowd of onlookers can be an amazing source of stimulus. A support team, whether present or not, is vital to the magnitude of the task.

Major marathons are well organized. Hundreds of volunteers assist in all aspects of the race. The organization is designed to keep runners focused on the challenge of the race and make all other aspects of it easy to deal with. Registration and distribution of packets are two prerace and race day activities. The packets contain information beneficial to the runner and usually include a runner's number and a map of the course. It may also contain a T-shirt, restaurant and lodging locations, and much other useful information.

Organizers position numerous volunteers along the course to shout time intervals at each mile marker so runners can be aware of their elapsed time. This enables them to calculate whether they are ahead or behind of their anticipated pace.

Water stops are another convenience. They are well placed and staffed with people who greet runners with cups of water or some type of power drink. Water stops enable runners to stay well hydrated without having to carry the weight of a valuable liquid. Some runners grab cups on the go from a volunteer without breaking stride; others may stop to help themselves. Some choose to carry their own preferred hydration in various types of containers.

Large marathons bring out local radio stations, sponsors, and other organizations willing to cheer on and encourage the runners in their effort. It's amazing how a cheer or a smile from a friendly face can lift a runner's spirit and distract from the pain.

In a race of this scope, surrounded by thousands of others, most serious runners choose to run alone. If the goal of the race is to obtain a personal best, runners must focus entirely on their training plan and apply it with their noblest effort. On the other hand, many runners choose to run because of peer influence. Those individuals are easy to spot because they usually lack a level of seriousness, which is easy to recognize. The purpose for their run is just social in nature. The need to be part of the group and not be outdone can result in serious consequences. Injury and regret can easily beset this type of runner.

God created us in such a way that relationships are vital to our being. His design placed in us the need to have a support group. Our accountability, however, is to Him, one on one. He, through His Holy Spirit, designed us in such a way that our best performance in life will be achieved only by operating according to His training program. No matter how lonely our run may seem, His desire is to be right there by our side. Remember, He has already run this course on our behalf, and we should draw from His expertise. Again, no matter how lonely our runs may be, we will always have a desire to share the ups and downs of our courses with someone. The concept of relationship is built into us by our

Creator, and we should develop it according to His design. We need the encouragement His Holy Spirit provides to stay focused on our course, while at the same time encouraging others to focus on their daunting runs. We certainly need to be encouraged by others as well.

The world and its failed system present numerous obstacles designed to entrap runners who have no relationship with their Creator. Without a relationship with Him, spiritual injury can be easily realized.

Our need for validation through relationships goes beyond the physical into the spiritual. We need approval and confirmation from not only our support teams here on Earth, but from our Creator as He indicates that we are on the right path, the pathway He has chosen for us. Support from His Spirit within our spirit has been made available to us through faith. He wants to not only support us; he wants to coach us through our real-time race experience of life. The writer of the book of Hebrews expressed the idea in these words:

> Let your conversation be without covetousness; and be content with such things as ye have: for he hath said, *I will never leave thee, nor forsake thee.*
>
> So that we may boldly say, The Lord is my helper, and I will not fear what man shall do unto me. (Hebrews 13:5–6)

In reference to our relationship with others and the support they give us, the same author said:

And let us consider one another to provoke unto
love and to good works:

Not *forsaking the assembling of ourselves together*,
as the manner of some is; but *exhorting one another*:
and so much the more, as ye see the day approaching.
(Hebrews 10:24–25)

Paul is believed to be the author of Hebrews by inspiration
of the Holy Spirit in his life. As such, these two scriptures fall in
line with Paul's way of thinking when compared to his use of a
running analogy. He is saying there can be a great deal of support
available in a group of spiritually minded people. We should be
cheering each other on in the spirit of truth. In my experience,
having someone available to encourage me while running through
a valley in my life is irreplaceable.

Because I am in the latter part of my run through life, I have
focused more on having the Holy Spirit be my coach—my Holy
Coach. I have paid attention, listened, and learned. For me, He is
now an ever-present perfect Coach. There is no one better than the
one who made me to know my strengths and weaknesses. I have
struggled to meet His expectations, and too often, I have failed. I
take confidence in the fact He has said He will never leave me or
forsake me. I keep my focus on the road ahead.

We are all His unique creations and have been given different
talents, abilities, and interests. Because of our individuality, we
respond differently to the many tests placed before us. Often, we
respond according to previous life experiences, and not necessarily
in God's desired way. Some of us struggle in areas of weakness that

the tempter is sure to exploit. The way we handle these encounters is often determined by the wisdom of the support group we belong to. Our spiritual growth is usually relative to our association with members of the five-fold ministry and other individuals who keep us accountable. As believers, we are all members of His body, serving different functions designed to reinforce the needs of others. Our willingness to share with and cheer on others as they experience their life runs can be vital to not only their victory but ours as well.

The ideas in the following paragraphs have been expressed in an earlier chapter; however, His guidance leads me to be repetitive at this point. Faith in Jesus qualifies us for His eternal kingdom while we are here on earth; subsequently, that gift of His grace provides us with a new starting line into His "eternal kingdom," which extends beyond this earthly life. Faith in Jesus and what He did for us at the time we first believed draws a new line on the pavement of life, so to speak. Imagine the number of spectators and supporters who could be present when you place your feet on your "eternal" starting line.

Paul, our primary reference in this discussion, was extremely familiar with athletics in his day. In Hebrews he described the crowd present in these words: "Wherefore seeing *we also are compassed about with so great a cloud of witnesses,* let us lay aside every weight, and the sin which doth so easily beset us, and let us run with patience the race that is set before us" (Hebrews 12:1)

The greatest support for runners in the "here and now" usually comes from their spouses and children. The amount of time needed to achieve the level of conditioning necessary to run such a challenging race is considerable. Six to eight hours of training per week is probably a very minimum. Relationships and success often develop hand in hand. The difficulty is being focused and dedicated to two objectives at the same time. Running extensively and having full support from your family can be quite a challenge.

God has spoken His desire for our success by the relationship pattern He has set for us in His Word. He wants to help us through our treacherous course called life! He is the primary help and support we need along the way. He has created us for this relationship. That need is built into who we are. It is stronger in some people than in others. Some struggle with adversity while others have distinct personality traits that thrive on adversity. Look at the words He used when speaking man into being: "And God said, Let us make man in our image, after our likeness" (Genesis 1:26).

Knowing we are created in His image and likeness leads me to conclude that this is so we can bond with Him, satisfying both His and our requirements for relationship. Consider these words spoken by Jesus: "And if I go and prepare a place for you, I will come again, and receive you unto myself; *that where I am, there ye may be also*" (John 14:3).

Because our discussion here is about having a support group, let us consider the wisdom of Solomon:

> *Two are better than one*; because they have a good reward for their labour.
>
> For if they fall, the *one will lift up his fellow*: but woe to him that is alone when he falleth; for he hath not another to help him up.
>
> Again, if two lie together, then they have heat: but how can one be warm alone?
>
> And if one prevail against him, two shall withstand him; and *a threefold cord is not quickly broken*. (Ecclesiastes 4:9–12)

The desire to be with and enjoy another's company is the basis for a good relationship. Good sound relationships with spouse and children are vital to compensate for the tremendous amount of time spent running. It is critical to have them involved with your running as much as possible. Without the strength of relationship, the time you spend running can be quite damaging to the family unit. You need to be very aware of the family members' needs and be creative in the way time is used for training. Dedicated runners should take extra special care to balance training time with the needs of their personal and closest support groups, their families.

Let us dive a bit deeper into that last scripture. Solomon ends in verse twelve by saying, "a threefold cord is not quickly broken." The third cord not identified in the first three verses is God, His Spirit. When He is the third party in any earthly relationship, that bond is on a sure path of success. He is the most important of the three cords: God, you, and your support group.

Another collection of supporters found in a marathon consists of our fellow runners. Most runners support and encourage each other on or off the course no matter how simple or elite their running level may be. Knowing the effort and training that goes into preparation almost always translates into a great respect and admiration for all who dare to take on the challenge. We are all seeking to give it our best effort and hear "well done" from onlookers.

The excitement of the race often spills over to nonrunners who are inspired to give it a try. Once this occurs, be ready to share your experience with these new recruits. You may well become their coach and source of support until they gain enough experience to find their own way. Dependence on you may go as far as running side by side with them in training or even during their entire first marathon.

As believers, we are all one family, one running club. The race that God has placed before us is what we have in common. Although our circumstances are quite different, we all run the vast distance of life. How well we run and what degree of success we achieve depends greatly on how much effort we put into it and how well we listen to the Word of our Coach along with the support of family members and fellow runners.

According to God, we are called upon to be disciples. That means we should help others in any way possible to see that God's training program is the only plan that provides success here and into eternity. When we encourage others to latch onto the confidence and trust we have experienced, He promises a guaranteed future reward for us. Paul expressed much of the same thought in Galatians:

> Be not deceived; God is not mocked: for whatsoever a man soweth, that shall he also reap.
>
> For he that soweth to his flesh shall of the flesh reap corruption; but *he that soweth to the Spirit shall of the Spirit reap life everlasting.*
>
> And let us not be weary in well doing: for in due season we shall reap, if we faint not. (Galatians 6:7–9)

Jesus recruited disciples who, in turn, recruited their own disciples. The result is proof in the mere fact that you and I are here today reflecting on the value of being a believer. A true believer knows there is only one way to win the race of life. We must encourage, edify, and disciple others along the course they run while we run our own.

Whether we find ourselves in a large or small community fellowship, we are duty bound to volunteer in areas where we can be of support to fellow believers (serious runners) as well as the ones who just got caught up in the excitement of the race and are searching for purpose and understanding in life. The ultimate coach for a new believer is the Holy Spirit. A secondary coach is a well-seasoned disciple who can guide and advise that runner according to God's Word. Our Creator knows His disciples better than anyone and will direct them to run according to their God-given interests, talents, and abilities. Jesus said:

> Go ye therefore, and teach all nations, baptizing them in the name of the Father, and of the Son, and of the Holy Ghost:
> *Teaching them to observe all things whatsoever I have commanded you*: and, lo, I am with you alway, even unto the end of the world. Amen. (Matthew 28:19–20)

Jesus has made available His Word as our source of faith so that we as believers can feed on it and replenish our reserves of faith, so desperately needed to carry us the distance. It is not just about us; it is also about the ones we run side by side with. An adage we all know says that misery loves company. The questions then become whose misery do we want to help carry, and are we building a relationship with this person so we can share the spirit of truth and joy? We should share the spirit of life with those around us and point them away from the spirit of confusion the world has placed on them.

A good disciple running his race should be able to look for better ways to reach uncommitted runners. Our commission in

Mark 16:15 is to "go ye" and seek runners who have no purpose or direction so they too can "receive the prize" upon completing their course.

Consider the encouragement we have received versus the support we can be to others.

Who is on your support team?

Are you willing to be a part of someone's support team cheering for his or her success?

What can we do to better nurture others who run with no purpose?

CHAPTER 9

MILE MARKERS

Miles and mile markers are important in training for a long run. They help us chronicle our actual progress by how much time it took to cover that distance. It is a simple calculation—how many minutes does it take to run a mile? This time becomes our benchmark that we strive to improve. Once we begin serious training, we should continue to chart our progress. Knowing our level of improvement after extended periods of serious workouts enables us to better formulate a targeted pace and time to complete the race before us.

Example: if you have been training at a pace of eight minutes per mile and have run several distances of twenty miles at that pace, then you can expect to run at that same or better for a complete marathon. The ability to run that distance at that pace plus the adrenaline from the excitement of the race will push you through the finish line. Establishing a good base of training over an extensive length of time is your key to readiness. Adrenalin created at the start, if carefully applied during the race, can supplement your training for the needed boost to exceed your expected pace and targeted time.

In a similar way, birthdays enable us to accurately reference specific times in our lives. They also act as natural indicators for expected performances levels for ourselves and others. Physical maturity and fitness combine for an expected higher level of performance up to the point where our bodies peak. As we use mile markers, many of us use age to look back and determine where we are in our natural run and what we have achieved up to this point. Often, such evaluations help us develop identifiable seasons in our lives that may have been productive or not. In this analogy of the marathon, mile markers are a close equivalent to age markers.

More important than our natural birthday is our "new birth" spiritual birthday. That marker becomes the fresh start so many of us need. Being able to mark the time of our new birth gives us an additional reference point to help us determine how seriously committed and purpose driven we have become while running with our Savior. Having that reference point alone can identify and liberate us from our many prior failures. Jesus did all the Father expected of Him here on Earth so we could have a new start with newness of life. Faith in Him is the initiator of that life, not mile markers or earthly wisdom. Jesus is not only the redeemer of our souls; He can also restore the time we have lost running away from Him. He created time but is not constrained by it. He wants us to maximize the amount of time we have left using His help. When we run side by side with Him, the mile markers seem to fly by.

Running competitively in the flesh can be very satisfying and uplifting to all who participate. Running in the Spirit enables our God-given purpose to develop according to His design. With a level of knowledge and maturity like Paul's, we can better serve and help direct others. Practicing our faith in His Word builds eternal endurance for us to power through the tough miles we experience here on Earth. When we are led by His Spirit, each mile marker yields some degree of result according to His design in and for us. It may be as simple as helping other believers get through to their next mile marker. Jesus said it this way: "And whosoever shall compel thee to go a mile, go with him twain" (Matthew 5:41).

If we do as Jesus has requested—go the extra mile—we will develop a stronger faith base within that endeavor. It is what we call ministry, not a burden, although it may be burdensome at times. Each extra effort enables us to "pick up our pace" and, in the long run, run stronger. These extra efforts build character and endurance, which yield a payoff for the latter miles of our lives. Day by day, mile by mile, we need to pay close attention to the coaching of the Holy Spirit who assures us a victorious pace.

Think about the ground you have covered and the miles still ahead.

Are you willing to look back at past mile markers and realistically check your progress?

Are you where you should be on your natural as well as your spiritual life course?

With the miles that loom before you, how much stronger can you run?

CHAPTER 10

WATER STOPS

Water stops are necessary for rehydration. During a marathon, a runner may lose as much as a quart of water per hour. This race is sufficiently long enough that, without adequate rehydration, a runner may collapse on the course or, at best, finish critically exhausted. Our bodies need the proper fuel for the task at hand. Our caloric intake needs to be measured and calculated along with hydration so that we can power through such a demanding course. It is important to load up on carbohydrates the week before and the evening prior to the event. Additionally, runners must be so hydrated that several bathroom calls may be made during the night before the race and in the morning prior to the start.

Race organizers place sufficient water stops and portable toilets at set distances to accommodate the runners who need to replenish body fuel as it is expended. Some runners opt to carry water bottles and energy bars to consume along the way, allowing their body to refuel with familiar fluids and calories. All runners should have a good plan with practiced techniques for keeping their bodies fueled prior to and during the entire event.

In the thick of the race, it takes technique and caution to drink, breathe, and run without choking. The same is true for our spiritual marathon. Knowing how to apply the truth we have learned can be a challenge for our flesh to accept. We are truly creatures of habit, and because of that, often the flesh will push back on any effort we make to change our training pace or direction. To operate properly—in a by-the-Book way—our spirit beings must be effectively hydrated with "living water" Jesus. In like manner, our spirit beings must operate on the caloric content that is provided by Jesus—the bread of life—otherwise, we may enter eternity emaciated. Our spirit beings demand the same care and attention that is demanded by our physical bodies. The parallel between the two is awesome to ponder.

According to Paul, the Word of God is our fuel for a true and robust race. In this life, whether you understand it or not, we run both physically and spiritually. Physically, we need to constantly fuel our bodies with high-quality food and proper hydration. We should focus on doing the same with our minds and spirits by seeking to consume knowledge and truth along the way.

God has made us three-part beings: body, soul (mind), and spirit. Your spirit is made to live eternally and should never be neglected. We are primarily unique spirit beings that need to grow just as our bodies do. In our society, too many people have ignored feeding their spirits, or in too many cases, have nourished them with junk food—the foolishness of the world. Is it any wonder that so many lives and the course they have run have been shortened by drugs, alcohol, and immorality? Many human spirits have been moved into despair by following the influences of society, which offer a false purpose of life. Hopelessness and suicide are needlessly common today. Paul offered another solution to our current problems in his letter to the Romans in which he said, "So then faith cometh by hearing, and hearing by the word of God" (Romans 10:17).

Faith in the one who calls himself "the bread of life" is the fuel and hydration our spirits can thrive on. Only God has the answer to every person's spiritual need, and it can be found at the water stops of His Word: "But without faith it is impossible to please him: for he that cometh to God must believe that he is, and that he is a rewarder of them that diligently seek him" (Hebrews 11:6).

Life is so demanding that we can deplete our faith-fuel easily as we run. As we stoke up on carbs and make multiple hydration stops, we must also consistently make similar stops in His Word in order to feed and replenish our spirit.

> Jesus answered and said unto her, If thou knewest the gift of God, and who it is that saith to thee, Give me to drink; thou wouldest have asked of him, and he would have given thee *living water*. (John 4:10)
>
> He that believeth on me, as the scripture hath said, out of his belly shall flow rivers of living water.
>
> But this spake he of the Spirit, which they that believe on him should receive. (John 7:38–39)

His Word says that faith in who He is furnishes us with a spiritual fuel and hydration that enables us to power through our races here on Earth. Like a good training program, discipline and sacrifice will pay off as we diligently and frequently seek Him while consuming His "living" Word. Serious believers can grab hold of a scripture during their race, and as runners hydrate on the run, they integrate it into their race effort without breaking stride, day after day.

John's race was the longest of the disciples' races, and he encountered many perils along the way. Here is his description of the course that was placed before him. Very few of us could run his course today:

> Are they ministers of Christ? (I speak as a fool) I am more; in labours more abundant, in stripes above measure, in prisons more frequent, in deaths oft.
>
> Of the Jews five times received I forty stripes save one.
>
> Thrice was I beaten with rods, once was I stoned, thrice I suffered shipwreck, a night and a day I have been in the deep;
>
> In journeyings often, in perils of waters, in perils of robbers, in perils by mine own countrymen, in perils by the heathen, in perils in the city, in perils in the wilderness, in perils in the sea, in perils among false brethren;
>
> In weariness and painfulness, in watchings often, in hunger and thirst, in fastings often, in cold and nakedness. (2 Corinthians 11:23–27)

John kept moving to his eternal reward not in His own strength, but by faith in the One who supplied him with strength. Jesus, through the Holy Spirit, said to John, "And he said unto me, It is done. I am Alpha and Omega, the beginning and the end. *I will give unto him that is athirst of the fountain of the water of life freely*" (Revelation 21:6)

God's Word was John's source of living water, the life source of his spirit. It was vital to him then, as it is to us today.

As a new believer or a nonbeliever, you may have to stop and contemplate on God's "Living Water," the nourishment of all life, before consuming it. Just as new runners may have to pause running to drink so they won't choke, so might new believers have to interrupt their old lives to properly fuel their new spirits. Hearing and understanding Jesus, the Living Water, will revive and propel faithful runners back to a correction in course leading them to a higher level of spiritual strength and endurance.

Do you have a plan to keep yourself fueled for a lifelong run?

When was the last time you took advantage of a water stop in God's Word?

Do you need to adjust the frequency of your stops to stay properly fueled?

Are you being careful to avoid the junk food the world offers as truth?

CHAPTER 11

UNEXPECTED EVENTS

All runners, at some point, encounter a surprise along the way. Experienced ones stay focused and ready to adjust their initial plan accordingly. Inexperience can easily cause runners to descend into a state of panic and confusion when they encounter an unexpected circumstance. No matter how well or how long you train, in the distance and scope of a race, a curve ball can be thrown your way. The focus behind intense training is to keep your body and mind working together as a team to accomplish the planned objective even if adjustments need to be made. Experience usually gives readiness to make that change on the fly.

Here are some of the ways a runner can be caught unaware. Officials may have decided to change the course you were familiar with and diligently prepared for. The weather may have taken an extreme turn. The pavement surface is not always the best and may offer extreme variations that create opportunities to trip. You may have planned to run solo in a sea of five thousand other runners when a friend you meet on race day asks if they can tag along at your pace. That can easily throw your planned pace off. Is it now your pace or theirs by default? Prior to the race someone may ask you to help them complete their first marathon. That kind of request can become more difficult during the actual race than crawling the entire distance. Keeping that someone moving at their pace, on the surface, would seem easy; but you probably trained at a faster pace, while their pace will cause you to be on your feet for a longer stretch of time. Such a request will take almost the same toll on you as it will on the friend who made the request. However, there is a great deal of satisfaction knowing you will cross the finish line together.

I have seen people get stomach sick along the way from a nervous reaction or altered eating habits or both. I have seen some running behind bushes because no portable toilets were in sight, or the line was too long. It is important to remember that no matter how well trained you are, your body can rebel under stress and unfamiliar circumstances.

Some obstacles may not even be real. You may overhear a conversation about an issue down the road that may be real or perhaps an exaggeration from an inexperienced runner. An alleged issue can often have the same effect as real one even though it may be nonexistent. The unfamiliar can be very confusing to the unprepared.

Satan is a master at creating doubt in our minds. He can take a partial truth and twist it in a certain way that can take our focus off our running plan and on to the deception. He is the master of deceit. For this reason, we must focus on the truth of God's Word because only this can help us triumph over all obstacles we encounter in our lives. Jesus explained it to His disciples in these words: "These things I have spoken unto you, that in me ye might have peace. *In the world ye shall have tribulation: but be of good cheer; I have overcome the world*" (John 16:33).

There are no sudden events that are too big for our Creator to handle through the faith and trust we have in Him. Even though we may trip and fall, He will always be there to pick us up to run again, even stronger. As our Coach, He has personally overcome the world of difficulties we live in. The unexpected does not exist in His realm. We must believe and trust only in His promises.

Some distractions are rather helpful. The larger and better-known events have planned diversions along the course such as grandmas dressed in aprons banging pots and pans, belly dancers doing their suggestive gyrations, high school cheerleaders and musical bands of every flavor cheering the runners on. Radio station mobile broadcasting units are sometimes positioned so that commentators can spot runners' numbers and announce their city and state of origin over the public address system. Distractions of this type are planned to take the runners' minds off the pain and agony they are experiencing and redirect their thoughts to more enjoyable sights and sounds.

When I was running the Houston Marathon, I heard someone say, "Look! President Bush." I turned to my right and, sure enough, there was President George H. W. Bush on the sidewalk. He had his white poodle in hand, and two secret service agents, one on either side of him. I could not pass up the opportunity. I turned around, ran up to him, shook his hand, and said: "Thank you for serving our country!"

Planned or unplanned, some distractions can help you temporarily forget the discomfort you are experiencing and can even add a benefit to the task. The important thing is to not lose focus on the purpose of your run: to win! It's important to be aware that the world system we live in—Satan's realm—is filled with confusion, partial truths, and outright lies. We live in this chaos and have no option but to try to steer clear of as many stumbling blocks as possible. To keep our focus, we must be knowledgeable of the truth and the source of that truth. His Word should be our source of truth by which we measure all obstacles in our paths. It is basic instruction from our Creator, giving us the ability to determine if we are correctly on course with our run or if we have been following lies brewed in the pit of hell.

In a marathon run, we have no way of knowing what unexpected event may await around the corner. It is the same with our life courses. No matter how well organizers prepare a course, there will always be unplanned incidents of some sort. We may think we have everything in our lives under control when, suddenly, that course will take an unexpected turn. Today more than ever, this has become a reality of life. Our society seems to have redefined norms that have existed since the beginning of time, especially if they were defined by God. With the certainty of such daily confusion, we need to constantly practice drawing upon our Coach's wisdom. He knows us better than we know ourselves. That wisdom was Solomon's request to God:

> I returned, and saw under the sun, that the race is not to the swift, nor the battle to the strong, neither yet bread to the wise, nor yet riches to men of understanding, nor yet favour to men of skill; but *time and chance happeneth to them all.*
>
> For *man also knoweth not his time*: as the fishes that are taken in an evil net, and as the birds that are caught in the snare; so are the sons of men snared in an evil time, when it falleth suddenly upon them.

This wisdom have I seen also under the sun,
and it seemed great unto me. (Ecclesiastes 9:11–13)

With all his wisdom, Solomon still failed as he took his focus off the One who had given it to him. When our lives, without warning, become difficult, we need to examine ourselves alongside God's Word. Are we following His lead, the lead of our Holy Coach? Or have we become complacent and distracted from His winning objective? We simply cannot allow ourselves to be found sitting on the curb of life unprepared to deal with the rest of our race. If we daily seek His guidance, we will be better able adjust to and overcome these unexpected events along the course. Thank God that He is a God of mercy! Our God can and often does mercifully redeem lost time along with our lack of solid faith in Him. No matter what surprises come our way, our Coach is always faithful and ready to help us as He helped Paul: "Holding forth the word of life; that I may rejoice in the day of Christ, that I have not run in vain, neither laboured in vain" (Philippians 2:16).

It is His desire to dwell in us as our ever-present, built-in guide. He wants to get us around, over, and through the obstacles in our life courses and lead us to victory.

Hereby know ye the Spirit of God: *Every spirit that confesseth that Jesus Christ is come in the flesh is of God:*

And *every spirit that confesseth not that Jesus Christ is come in the flesh is not of God: and this is that spirit of antichrist,* whereof ye have heard that it should come; and even now already is it in the world.

Ye are of God, little children, and have overcome them: because *greater is he that is in you, than he that is in the world*. (1 John 4:2–4)

With a renewed mind, we give Him full control to not only help us avoid many of the unexpected events along our course, but to empower us to be in control with Him when we face them. Remember: when Jesus walked the Earth as a man, He faced similar obstacles to the ones we encounter and more. He overcame all of them on our behalf. By His Spirit, who is now our Coach, we have been empowered to do the same—overcome obstacles as we seek and listen to His lead. He not only wants to direct us through the course we run, but He also wants to be our escort and tour guide through this life, providing gifts of provision and protection along the way.

When we come to faith in Jesus, His Spirit comes to dwell in us. At that point, we should open our hearts and allow Him to clean it out in such a way that He can retrain us in the way we should run our race. His experience will help us stay on the course He has set before us.

How well can you handle the unexpected?

Have Satan's distractions and lies taken your focus off the purpose of your life journey?

Do you seek the fundamental knowledge to know the difference between the truth and lies?

Do you have a Coach to help you make needed adjustments in your run?

CHAPTER 12

THE WALL AND A
SECOND WIND

There is a phenomenon in long-distance runs called "the wall." You sometimes hear runners refer to "hitting the wall." This effect upon a runner depends greatly on the individual's overall condition, including physical fitness and mental preparation plus the amount of energy that has been depleted. The wall is hidden, but it becomes overwhelmingly present when all the conditions are met.

Runners hit the wall when they reach a point in the race where they have maxed out their physical stamina, caloric fuel, hydration, or a combination of these. When the wall presents itself, it seems too tall to climb over, too wide to run around, and too heavy to move out of the way. Some runners collapse or quit at this point, and some do not have the wherewithal to stop or just slow down. It will muddle runners' minds in a serious way. Without the proper knowledge of what is happening to their bodies, runners can end up in an ambulance headed to the first aid station. Others who begin to sense what is taking place in their bodies will rationalize by seeking hydration and power bars or even slowing their pace.

Runners who choose to slow their pace should continue to move, at least walking toward the finish line at their best possible pace. Running through the wall is the only way to conquer it once it presents itself. The key is to keep moving so muscles do not tighten up, which produces more incapacitation and additional pain. Continued movement keeps runners' muscles loose, warm, and most of all, moving in the right direction. Once runners make it through the wall, completion of the course can still be accomplished. Recovery will usually be partial at this point, and pace will certainly be slower than before. Better trained and more experienced runners may not undergo or even fear the possibility of a wall obstructing their path. They know from experience what it takes to run through it and have the understanding and vision of how to properly deal with it.

As humans, we often have experiences that replicate the effect of hitting a wall. Have you ever reached a point where you feel you can no longer move forward? Everything in front of you refuses to move out of the way. Have you been overwhelmed, worn out, weighted down, or for some other reason feel as if you cannot take another step? Have you ever wanted to just quit and raise your hands in total submission to the circumstances at hand? The stresses of life in our culture, as well as the ones we put on ourselves by the choices we make, can be burdensome and seem unmovable at times. We have an answer.

The remedy in a marathon is having a good race plan, running at a trained-for pace, and having a well-fueled body. Preparation of this type can totally prevent the "wall" effect and can really provide a "second wind" of effort when others are struggling.

Our spiritual parallel to this is a studious consumption of God's Word, the knowledge of His promises, and the application of its provision. His Spirit says that, if we are fortified with His protective covering, we have no reason to quit or fail. Paul said we must never give up standing against evil and the walls that suddenly appear in our lives. He explained it this way: "Wherefore take unto you the whole armour of God, that ye may be able to withstand in the evil day, and having done all, to stand. Stand therefore..." (Ephesians 6:13–14)

The amount of strength we have available to run through the walls of life is in direct proportion to the amount of faith we have in God, who provides our essentials in these evil days. He is our Coach who runs with us, directing and moving us in His strength. We must stand in faith and knowledge of His truth for Him to do it.

Whether runners hit the wall or not, many do experience what is called a "second wind." It can be a recovery from hitting wall, when their bodies have had time to replenish some of the fuel they have depleted, or it can be an extra burst that results from a reserve that originates from within. It is a second burst of adrenaline that powers them through to the finish line. This effect is much easier to access if no wall has been experienced and the runner's pace has been consistent to his or her level of training. It is as if the body searches its inner parts and emerges with a stash of momentum to fuel a second attempt at success. The well-trained runner will always welcome that "second wind" and will draw upon its benefits during the relentless final miles of the race.

God has provided for all runners the perfect solution to the cares and stresses of life that repeatedly run us into walls. As believers, we are all given new life by a new birth along with the perfect Coach to guide us through our courses. "Newness of life" is God's provision for a powerful second wind. The move of the Spirit upon us is often referred to as the wind of the Spirit. A renewed spirit with a changed heart is to us like a breeze from heaven on an extremely hot day. With our changed heart, God gives us new direction with the guidance and power to run to our finish lines as winners. Nicodemus was introduced to this truth when he came to Jesus inquiring about eternal life:

> There was a man of the Pharisees, named Nicodemus, a ruler of the Jews:

The same came to Jesus by night, and said unto him, Rabbi, we know that thou art a teacher come from God: for no man can do these miracles that thou doest, except God be with him.

Jesus answered and said unto him, Verily, verily, I say unto thee, *Except a man be born again, he cannot see the kingdom of God.*

Nicodemus saith unto him, How can a man be born when he is old? can he enter the second time into his mother's womb, and be born?

Jesus answered, Verily, verily, I say unto thee, *Except a man be born of water and of the Spirit,* he cannot enter into the kingdom of God.

That which is born of the flesh is flesh; and that which is born of the Spirit is spirit.

Marvel not that I said unto thee, Ye must be born again.

The wind bloweth where it listeth, and thou hearest the sound thereof, but canst not tell whence it cometh, and whither it goeth: so is every one that is born of the Spirit. (John 3:1–8)

The barriers we face in our lives test how well we have prepared for the challenge. Some trials come to us through choices we have made; others, by circumstances around us. If we are well versed in the Word of God and have studied to show ourselves approved with experience in our faith stand, no wall will be able to hold us back. Preparation according to His Word is vital to our successful stand. It will produce in us a "spiritual second wind" as often as we need it so we can continue our run in faith.

As a ruler of the Jews, Nicodemus should have known these two scriptures:

> But this shall be the covenant that I will make with the house of Israel; After those days, saith the Lord, I will put my law in their inward parts, and write it in their hearts; and will be their God, and they shall be my people. (Jeremiah 31:33)

> And I will give them one heart, and I will put a new spirit within you; and I will take the stony heart out of their flesh, and will give them an heart of flesh:
>
> That they may walk in my statutes, and keep mine ordinances, and do them: and they shall be my people, and I will be their God. (Ezekiel 11:19–20)

When we are "born again," as Jesus told Nicodemus, God renews our hearts and puts them in alignment with His Spirit. Simultaneously, He gives new life to our formerly lifeless spirits. This is all accomplished by the same Holy Spirit that raised Jesus from the grave. With all its power, it raises us from eventual death into eternal life with Him. By the grace of God, Jesus paid the price that we might be able to cross our life finish line into eternity with Him. At the point of our new birth, God places within us His reserves, which enable us to power through the walls we face.

Those reserves are activated by faith to give us a much needed "second wind."

Unrepented sin, in due course, brings us to the wall of death. The Word of God says, "The wages of sin is death" (Romans 6:23). Faith in Jesus pulls us away from those walls and sets us back on our courses with a strong second wind in our lungs and at our backs. His Word keeps us faithful and confident, able to face more unforeseen challenges. The strength of our relationship with our Holy Coach keeps us from having to sit on the curb of life watching other runners go by. Faith enables us to keep running or walking in the right eternal direction.

If you find yourself on the curb of life, get up, speak His Word in faith, and trust Him to coach you to the finish line, step by step, mile by mile.

As a true man of faith, Jeremiah asked this question: "If thou hast run with the footmen, and they have wearied thee, then how canst thou contend with horses? and if in the land of peace, wherein thou trustedst, they wearied thee, then how wilt thou do in the swelling of Jordan?" (Jeremiah 12:5).

We must trust in the Lord to lead us through the trials of life. Paul confronted us with these words:

> Knowing that he which raised up the Lord Jesus shall raise up us also by Jesus, and shall present us with you.
>
> For all things are for your sakes, that the abundant grace might through the thanksgiving of many redound to the glory of God.

> For which cause we faint not; but though our outward man perish, yet the inward man is renewed day by day.
>
> For our light affliction, which is but for a moment, worketh for us a far more exceeding and eternal weight of glory. (2 Corinthians 4:14–17)

Newness of life—that "born again spirit"—was designed by God to give us a second wind no matter where we are during the course of our run. He is by our side coaching us to the finish as we keep seeking His guidance: "But without faith it is impossible to please him: for he that cometh to God must believe that he is, and that *he is a rewarder of them that diligently seek him*" (Hebrews 11:6).

Without the new birth spoken of by Jesus, the one heart spoken of in Ezekiel, and the heart in Jeremiah with God's law written upon it, it is impossible to finish our race as winners. However, with faith in God, we have the second wind of His Spirit at our backs to not only finish our race, but to finish it strong.

Are you looking for joy in your weariness?

Is there a reserve of faith in you that can fuel you through any unforeseen wall?

Do you have a training plan to develop a stronger faith that will help you better face the barricades ahead?

Are you seeking God for a much needed "second wind" in your life?

CHAPTER 13

FINISH LINE

This section is about the finish line—the point at which we finish the race. It is the place at which we measure how well we did with the challenges we trained for. I am sure you have noticed that there has been no specific chapter for the starting line. The traditional marathon has a fixed starting line. Runners are challenged to run 26.2 miles to the finish line. We will return to the finish line in the next few paragraphs. For now, let us look back and study the starting line a little closer.

In chapter 9, on the subject of mile markers, we compared our birthday mile markers to mile markers in a marathon. In birthday increments, we usually measure our growth physically and mentally. The dimensions that we often overlook, neglect, and in some cases purposely avoid are our spirit and its growth. God has made special provision for our spirit to be whole and complete. This was necessary because, when Adam sinned in the garden, he and Eve died spiritually. Before that incident, their spirits were alive and clothed in the glory of God. Their newfound nakedness revealed the truth of God's warning command. From that point, all of humanity has been born in innocence with spirits lacking true life. God so loved humanity that he provided a way out of death into true life, His life.

Our entry into eternal life with the Father comes only through faith in Jesus. When He walked the Earth, He spoke these words to His apostles, specifically Thomas: "Jesus saith unto him, I am the way, the truth, and *the life: no man cometh unto the Father, but by me*"(John 14:6).

Our only entry into eternal life with our Creator is by faith in Jesus and his payment for our sins on the cross. This brings us to what believers know and what Jesus himself described to Nicodemus as the new birth—to be "born again." We have mentioned this term before, but it deserves more explanation. When we, as believers, first come to faith in Jesus, our spirits are regenerated into newness of life by the Holy Spirit. An amazing miracle takes place. We are given a new starting line in our race through life on Earth. No matter what we are found guilty of, God forgives us when we confess our sins and place our faith in Jesus and the price He paid for them.

By our faith, God provides a new starting line for us. There is no given parameter in time, only that we must come to faith before our physical death. The thief on the cross who put his faith in Jesus ran a short race of faith that day. In the power of his faith, Jesus told him he would be with Him in Paradise that day. Many believers come to faith early in life and run in the Spirit of God year after year; others, like the thief, do so just before the moment of death.

Believer's experience two births here on this Earth. First is the physical birth by the water of a mother's womb. The second is the spiritual birth by faith in Jesus. This second birth is, by comparison, our second starting line. It guarantees that, when we cross our physical finish line, our reward will be eternal life.

Let us dig down a little deeper into this comparison. God, in His infinite wisdom, gave us free will. His love reflects His desire for us to choose to run to Him and with Him in His strength instead of running in our own limitations. He gave the life of His Son so you and I could do just that. We could say it cost Him everything. He has paid our entry fee to eternal life with His blood. It costs us nothing but our faith. We need to believe that He is who he says He is and that He has paid the price to redeem our sinful humanity. When we place our trust and faith in Him, He draws the spiritual starting line we have been discussing in the sands of Heaven. This spiritual new birth produces in us a change of heart and a desire to complete our race in a manner that is pleasing to Him. It is available to all at any given time in their physical span of years. It is a choice we make by the eye-opening revelation of God's amazing grace and love, through the good news of the gospel. We can choose to follow after God with His help or stay on the path leading to destruction. That decision should be made sooner than later.

Let us return this discussion to our earthly finish line. And read the words of Paul to Timothy.

> *I have fought a good fight, I have finished my course, I have kept the faith:*

Henceforth there is laid up for me a crown of righteousness, which the Lord, the righteous judge, shall give me at that day: and not to me only, but unto all them also that love his appearing.

Do thy diligence to come shortly unto me. (2 Timothy 4:7–9)

Approaching the finish line in a marathon creates in most runners a confidence and encouragement to keep going and finish as strong as possible. It produces the last burst of adrenaline that comes from knowing that, if the runner was able to work through twenty plus miles, he or she can certainly do a few more yards! Crossing over that line gives runners a sense of victory, completion, and satisfaction that is difficult to explain. After months and months of training, intensively following a workout schedule, and anxiously awaiting race day, the task is finally complete. Time for some well-deserved rest.

Houston - Tenneco Marathon.
January 26, 1998.

When runners cross that finish line, they display a variety of emotions, especially first-time marathon runners. Most express joy and some level of unbelief over what they have just accomplished. No matter how much pain and weakness they may be experiencing, there is great satisfaction mixed into their exhaustion. At that point, it is common for some runners to conclude they will never do it again, or question why they even did it in the first place. Later, once their body has healed, their minds may perhaps say, "I can do this again."

Once their emotions have returned to normal and their bodies have rested and started their healing process, casual running is necessary to retain a base of conditioning. This should not be strenuous, and is done to keep the muscles loose, strong, and at the level they were prior to the marathon.

In due time, most runners muster up the will to do another

marathon and seek to improve upon their best time, which is called a personal best. Most runners consider themselves middle-of-the pack runners. These are average runners who run well and finish well but will never break any record except their own personal best time.

Elite runners, on the other hand, run for a different purpose and possess greater levels of talent even though they run the same course you and I run. They compete for cash, for trophies, and for sponsorships. Middle-of-the pack runners run competitively against themselves or friends, always trying to improve their time. One year I bettered my best time by one second. Considering all the training runs—approximately fifteen hundred miles—on the same course one year later, even one second better is still better. Accept success any way it comes to you. Consistency is good; persistence is better.

God's desire is for us to achieve a personal best every time we hit the pavement in this life. He is there for us. His running program for our race is His Word. We should seek daily to maximize the gifts He has given us by training hard and building a close relationship with His Spirit, our Coach. Relationships in life are built through sharing and listening. This is no different with the way the Holy Spirit wants to coach and guide us through the life course we have been placed on. One day we will be asked to account for how well we have applied each gift He has given us. Our answer will be no better than how well we have applied His Word in our lives.

Anyone you ask wants to receive the ultimate prize of eternal life that we all know as heaven. This spiritual passage must be accomplished by the spirit of the individual leaving the flesh here on Earth and moving into eternity, its real home. Crossing that finish line is not always easy or pleasant. The flesh we live in must die for that to happen. I have not found anyone yet who looks forward to that. Usually, many physical challenges are associated with the process. The fear of death is the greatest fear known to humanity. God has provided good news. Death has been overcome by the life that Jesus lived, the way He died, and because He was resurrected. He crossed His finish line to make a way for us to follow: "These things I have spoken unto you, that in me ye might have peace. In the world ye shall have tribulation: but be of good cheer; *I have overcome the world*" (John 16:33).

The way of the world leads to death, and He said He overcame the world for us. Joy comes to us through the relationship we have with our Creator-Savior, which enables us to approach our end in confidence and faith, knowing our reward is just across the line.

In the same way runners finish a marathon, many people finish their life races well depleted physically while they are still searching for purpose. The wisdom in God's Word provides a plan for our lives, and with a careful ear to hear our coach's direction, we can finish strong, joyfully depleted, with the confidence that we gave it our best.

In addition, a burst of spiritual adrenaline is available not just during the race, but also as we near the finish line. Digging deep, we will find more faith in the bottomless depth of God's Word; however, we must stay focused on His purpose and continue our run. The strength we need is there. The supply of this strength is not dependent on our conditioning; it is based on His love for us, His grace. In Isaiah, His spiritual adrenaline is described in these words:

> He giveth power to the faint; and to them that have no might he increaseth strength.
>
> Even the youths shall faint and be weary, and the young men shall utterly fall:
>
> But they that wait upon the LORD shall renew their strength; they shall mount up with wings as eagles; they shall run, and not be weary; and they shall walk, and not faint. (Isaiah 40:29–31)
>
> Fellow runners let's cross that line with our heads high looking for the prize before us and seeking to hear these words: "His lord said unto him, *Well done, thou good and faithful servant*: thou hast been faithful over a few things, I will make thee ruler over many things: enter thou into the joy of thy lord" (Matthew 25:21).

Address what you should anticipate.

Are you nearing your finish line but still wondering what comes next?

Do you train for this life run only, or can you see an eternal reward ahead?

Is eagerness moving you to the finish line of life by seeking your personal best?

CHAPTER 14

THE PRIZE AND THE REWARD

All finishers of a marathon receive a prize packet containing items like a finisher's T-shirt, a mug, a medal, a photo or two, and other commercial items. Basically, these are things of little to no value; they are just mementos that provoke memories of the time and painful effort that went into the preparation for the race as well as the race itself.

Some people train a whole year focusing on that one event. Completing a marathon in good shape and in a reasonable amount of time is very satisfying and a definite confidence builder. The self-discipline needed to accomplish a challenge like that is hard to imagine by the average nonrunner. Other than improved physical health and satisfaction of meeting the trial's demand, we should ask: What value does it serve in the big picture of my life? What benefit can result from all the years I spent running? These were the questions I asked myself when I started looking back at the time and effort, I expended in order to run well.

There is only one official winner in the marathon; however, everyone who finishes is a real winner because of the overall scale of the task. The dedication and persistence required helps develop in the runner the attitude of a winner.

God has placed in the test and scale of our life runs the potential of eternal benefit, not just value in the here and now. Paul encouraged us to run, and not just to run, but to run to win the prize: "Know ye not that they which run in a race run all, but one receiveth the prize? *So run, that ye may obtain*" (1 Corinthians 9:24).

The prize that he referred to is eternal life and all that goes with it. He went on to say that, as true disciplined winners, we should seek a crown that is incorruptible. Anything incorruptible is designed to be eternal, with no end, perfect in its existence outside of the realm of time. Such a prize is of limitless value: "And every man that *striveth for the mastery* is *temperate in all things*. Now they do it to obtain a *corruptible crown*; but we *an incorruptible*" (1 Corinthians 9:25).

How do we obtain such a prize, and what exactly is it? We obtain the prize by being "in Christ." By faith, we place our trust in Him knowing He has already run this race on our behalf. We can say we are winners by proxy. We must remember this is totally a spiritual victory. It is a change of heart, a "born-again" victory, a victory by the regeneration of our spirit by faith in His Spirit. When our spirit is revived into the life of His Spirit, the two become one as in a marriage. By faith, we become winners because He became the ultimate winner in the way He lived a sinless life. He ran His race in perfection. By His life and death on the cross, He paid the price for our sin.

No matter where you are in your life or how long it took you to get there, or even the condition in which you find yourself, His Holy Spirit will run side by side with you if you place your faith in Jesus. The facts and past failures of your life are not important to Him. He obtained your incorruptible prize by His death upon the cross, and He wants you to claim it as your own before you cross over your earthly finish line. Placing your faith and trust in Jesus guarantees you the incorruptible crown Paul talked about.

Again, our most important qualification is that we finish our race, "in Christ." In Romans, Paul said: "There is therefore now no condemnation to them which are in Christ Jesus, who walk not after the flesh, but after the Spirit" (Romans 8:1).

John said it almost the same way. If we run according to God's preordained course, we are guaranteed to receive the ultimate prize.

> "Let that therefore abide in you, which ye have heard from the beginning. If that which ye have heard from the beginning shall remain in you, ye also shall continue in the Son, and in the Father.
>
> And this is the promise that *he hath promised us, even eternal life.* (1 John 2:24–25)

Eternal life is our prize as promised to us by the Father. Discipline and obedience to His Word are parts of a growth process that builds in us a spiritual endurance as we grow into faithful commitment to Him. Our promised crown is personal and an irreplaceable eternal one; it is unlike cheap medals and trophies we might be awarded here on Earth. Our eternal reward as promised has no comparability in value to any fleshly achievement we may gain in this life.

The Holy Spirit is our Coach and has promised to never leave our side. If we follow His training plan by standing on His Word and run our race seeking the prize, we win! See how this is stated in the letter to the Hebrews:

> Let your conversation be without covetousness; and be content with such things as ye have: for he hath said, *I will never leave thee, nor forsake thee.*
>
> So that we may boldly say, The Lord is my helper, and I will not fear what man shall do unto me. (Hebrews 13:5–6)

His promises and gifts are many. His training plan for you is personally designed upon the talents and abilities He has placed in you. Be content with these gifts and work hard to develop them. How well you run in your uniquely personal gifts is a challenge. Remember, He offers forgiveness for failures along the way. He wants your focus to be forward looking, not backward looking. Luke expressed much of the same idea with these words:

> And that servant, which knew his lord's will, and prepared not himself, neither did according to his will, shall be beaten with many stripes. But he that knew not, and did commit things worthy of stripes, shall be beaten with few stripes.

For unto *whomsoever much is given, of him shall be much required*: and to whom men have committed much, of him they will ask the more. (Luke 12:47–48)

Paul, in a letter to the church at Philippi, used the same athletic language to encourage their need to persevere and not give up. He challenged them to keep pressing forward to the incorruptible prize. No matter where we find our self in this life's run, we must do likewise. He stated it this way:

> Brethren, I count not myself to have apprehended: but this one thing I do, forgetting those things which are behind, and reaching forth unto those things which are before,
>
> *I press toward the mark* [finish line] for *the prize* of the high calling of God in Christ Jesus.
>
> Let us therefore, as many as be perfect, be thus minded: and if in anything ye be otherwise minded, God [our Coach] shall reveal even this unto you. (Philippians 3:13–15; "finish line" and "our coach" added)

Paul was consistent in his language, images, and messages throughout his writings. In 1 Corinthians, the main text for this analogy, he said: "Know ye not that they which *run in a race* run all, but one receiveth the prize? So run, that *ye may obtain*" (1 Corinthians 9:24).

In Ephesians, he said that, as believers, we have already been assigned a seat at the winners' table. Heaven is waiting in anticipation of a big celebration when we arrive to claim our prize: "Even when we were dead in sins, hath quickened us together with Christ, (by grace ye are saved;) And hath raised us up together, and *made us sit together in heavenly places* in Christ Jesus" (Ephesians 2:5–6).

What is the greatest prize any person can ever achieve?

Looking at what He provides for us here, how much more is prepared for us there?

Have you imagined the spiritual prizes you will receive for finishing a well-run race?

Are His promises encouragement enough to help you run better?

CHAPTER 15

IN CONCLUSION

We all live life "on the run" however long our span of years may be. We all carry baggage that often hinders our forward progress. With good training found in the Word of our Creator, we can discard unnecessary weight and run more efficiently. His desire is that we run the exact course He has set us on and run at a pace we can sustain for the distance. He provides all the support and direction we need if we only seek it. He is present when things do not go as they should. When we fall, He is nearby to pick us up and brush us off so we can run again. Our assurance in Him is that He will be there to hand us the trophy of eternal life with Him when we cross our finish lines.

Our courses are similar yet different with diverse experiences along the way. Have you had time to consider why you were born to run at this time in history? Why not at some time in the past or perhaps in the future?

These are the questions I asked myself at the beginning of the last chapter. What is the value of this running knowledge in the big picture of my life? And what benefit can result from all the years I spent running?

These are my thoughts: God created each one of us specifically with a unique personality, special talents, and the potential to play a specific role in His production show called *Time*.

Understand that God is a Spirit and is eternal. He not only exists inside and outside of time, but He created it all. He fashioned this production so the curtain could rise to reveal the first day of creation: "And the earth was without form, and void; and darkness was upon the face of the deep. And the Spirit of God moved upon the face of the waters. And God said, Let there be light: and there was light" (Genesis 1:2–3).

Likewise, it will close after the final scene of His return. To paraphrase Paul, we run the race that is placed before us. God has given us the freedom to follow or not follow His script and to interface with others who have that same choice. Because of those freedoms, He has had to rewrite the entire production several times and will do so again before the final curtain falls.

It is our duty as actors on His stage to follow the script as stated in His Word to the best of our ability and at the same time draw upon His present support.

I have reached an age where I can look back and ask, what have I contributed to God's overall objective? Are my interactions making a positive difference to others who are running their race or playing their roles? I believe I am getting better at this, but I still have a way to go. I have many more questions than answers.

As I stated at the beginning of this book, I spent much time during the younger part of my life running. For the better part of twenty-five years, I spent about 250 hours per year running. That is probably the reason for the good health I experience today. Because it was such a driving force in my life, I believe there had to be more value in it than just health. Perhaps there was spiritual reason behind it as well. Conceivably, God has used some of my experiences to speak to you. Maybe the time I spent running has helped you understand your need to get in better spiritual condition for the eternity that is still ahead for both of us.

I have described my experiences during training and running the physical 26.2-mile marathon. I see many parallels between that, and the way God wants us to live and run spiritually. The marathon is as tough and demanding as life itself. If I could have afforded a personal coach then, I would have wanted him to be just like the spiritual Coach I now have. He is loving, honest, and wise, holding me accountable to His high standards. Truth be known, we all have such a coach in our Savior Jesus and His Holy Spirit if we want Him. Let us learn to live in Him and follow His daily training.

My life objective at this point is to be in the same mindset of Paul as I begin to approach my finish line:

> I have fought a good fight, I have finished my course, I have kept the faith:
>
> Henceforth there is laid up for me a crown of righteousness, which the Lord, the righteous judge, shall give me at that day: and *not to me only, but unto all them also that love his appearing.* (2 Timothy 4:7–8).

What experiences can you share, and what role does God play in your life?

Our race is not yet complete. Time for course corrections still exists.

With the miles we have left, let us pay closer attention to our Coach's voice.

Printed in the United States
By Bookmasters